How to create
and develop
a Thinking Classroom

Mike Fleetham

Acknowledgements

I want to thank two groups of people for their help in producing this book.

The children:
Class 3F (2000–1) of Fernhurst Junior School, Southsea, for allowing me to teach them how to think; and Class 4F (2001–2) of Paulsgrove Primary School, Portsmouth, for showing me how intelligent they are.

The grown-ups:
Lucy and Jo for enthusiasm and proof-reading; Cathy and Corin at LDA for care, attention and expert help; Doug for opening up the world of teaching to me; Chris for encouraging me to write this book.

Dedication

For Ella and Arthur

Contributor profile

Dr Tamara Russell conducts research in neuroscience and emotion at King's College, London. But, unknown to most, she lives a secret life, moonlighting as an agony aunt for educators trying to make sense of brain-based teaching.

Permission to photocopy
This book contains materials which may be reproduced by photocopier or other means for use by the purchaser. The permission is granted on the understanding that these copies will be used within the educational establishment of the purchaser. The book and all its contents remain copyright. Copies may be made without reference to the publisher or the licensing scheme for the making of photocopies operated by the Publisher's Licensing Agency.

The right of Mike Fleetham to be identified as the author of this work has been asserted by him in accordance with sections 77 and 78 of the Copyright, Designs and Patents Act 1988.

Every effort has been made to obtain permission for the inclusion in this book of quoted material. Apologies are offered to anyone whom it has not been possible to contact.

How to create and develop a Thinking Classroom
LL01716
ISBN 1 85503 378 X
© Mike Fleetham
Cover illustration © Peter Wilks
Inside illustrations © David Pattison
All rights reserved
First published 2003
Reprinted 2004 (June, December)

Printed in the UK for LDA
Abbeygate House, East Road, Cambridge CB1 1DB UK

Contents

Contents

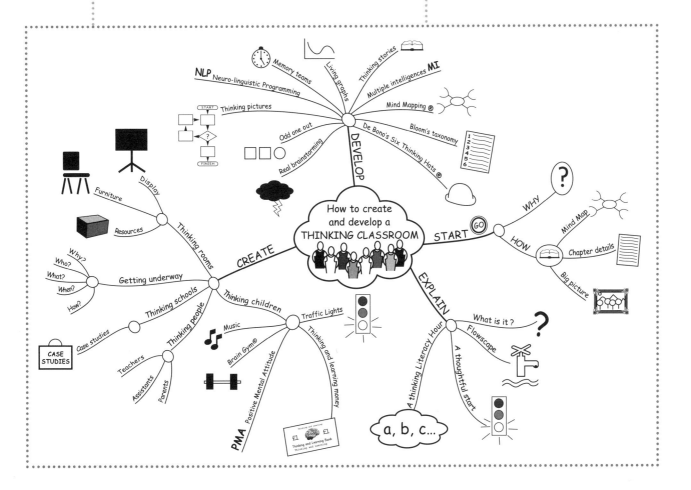

Foreword

As our new century unfolds we are witnessing many wonderful opportunities in the face of some difficult challenges. The rise of the individual and globalisation are the most prominent issues. More than ever before we now have the chance to know who we are and to understand our place in a shrinking world. But the speed of change is frightening. What skills and knowledge must we develop to keep up? How can we adapt and thrive when there is so much to learn? How do we survive as the world transforms before our very eyes?

One answer to these questions is simple. We must think. We must engage with what's going on around us. We must evaluate it; create it; then take control. That way we are in flow with the changing world, rather than being its spectators.

In this short and practical book you will find seeds of thought which you can plant in the minds of those you teach. As our curricula shift away from prescription and testing, and thankfully on to creativity and respect for different ways of learning, we need signposts to point the way. You will find them here. Use them to help transform your learners into thinkers who create, challenge, evaluate and make decisions; people who will succeed in the twenty-first century because you have given them the tools of thinking that they need.

C. Branton Shearer, PhD
President, MI Research and Consulting
Kent, Ohio, May 2003

Chapter 1
Start here

Look out for these symbols throughout the book:

○ Quotation

...we are bundles of thought in a thinking universe. And thought has the power to transform.
Deepak Chopra

○ Book/article/resource

How to Create and Develop a Thinking Classroom,
Mike Fleetham, LDA, 2003

○ Website

www.aspiroweb.co.uk

There are three ways to read this book:

○ Mind Map;
○ contents page;
○ cover to cover.

How to read this book

This book has been written by a teacher for teachers. It is a hands-on manual which should become dog-eared, not dusty. It is about thinking and learning, and it respects the different ways you may want to think and learn. So here are three ways to read it.

① If you want an overview first, study the Mind Map on the contents page.
② If you want to begin somewhere specific look at the headings on the contents page. The page numbers will direct you to chapters where references to articles, books, organisations and websites invite you to find out more.
③ If you want the full picture, with all the detail, examples and theory, read the main text.

There are four chapters in this book. Chapter 1 (where you are now) is an introduction that explains why thinking is so popular at the moment. Chapter 2 answers the question 'What is a Thinking Classroom?'

Chapter 3 describes what you have to do to make your classroom a Thinking Classroom. It gives practical ways to create a thinking environment and ethos and will develop your own thinking about how you want to teach.

In Chapter 4, you will find out how to develop your Thinking Classroom by working, learning and thinking in different ways. This section is full of practical thinking tools linked to the National Curriculum, the National Numeracy and Literacy Strategies and Qualifications and Curriculum Authority schemes of work – and all you will need to get going is a photocopier.

Scattered throughout the book are questions and answers about the brain and how to get the best from it. Our resident neuro-aunt, Dr Tamara Russell, will help you to see how the findings of neuroscience can help learning and thinking in the classroom.

I don't want to give you any extra work to do. I do want to share my enthusiasm, classroom experience and ideas with you. I want to help you get more from your pupils by thinking about *their* thinking; and to get more from your role as an educator by thinking about *your* thinking. But none of this should be at the expense of your family or free time. Everything in this book should be carried out as an enrichment to or replacement for what you already do, not as an addition.

If the curriculum content you have to deliver is a tasty three-course meal, then the skills of thinking and learning presented in this book are the knife and fork with which to eat it.

[we are] trying to graft the tools of the 21st century on to an educational model designed to service a 19th-century industrial economy.
Gordon Dryden and Jeanette Voss

The Learning Revolution,
Gordon Dryden and Jeanette Voss,
NEP, 2001

www.thelearningweb.net

Where your talents and the needs of the world cross, there lies your vocation.
Aristotle

Why you should read this book

'Brain-based teaching', 'individual learning styles', 'multiple intelligences', 'thinking skills', 'brain-friendly classrooms', 'accelerated learning', 'VAK' – how many of these have you heard in the last three months? What are they and do they have a place in the primary school classroom? I think they do.

A better grasp of how our brains grow and learn is starting to influence the way we teach. Neuroscience allows us to watch our brains at work and see which parts do what. New imaging techniques can show us which areas of the brain fire when we speak or sing, when we listen to music or when we learn something new. We know that each brain thinks and learns in a different way. For teachers, this knowledge is invaluable because, in theory, we can match our teaching to the exact needs of each child. In practice things are very different. How can we find the time and resources to get these innovations off the ground in a workable way?

Global trends in the ways we work, relax and learn demand changes in young people. At the age of 35, I am embarking on my third career. My own children could well change jobs up to eight times during their working lives. In our evolving world the ability to think is fast becoming more desirable than any fixed set of skills and knowledge. We need problem solvers, decision makers and innovators. And to produce them, we need new ways to teach and learn. We need to prepare our children for their future, not for our past. On this journey of preparation, we will have the chance not only to reclaim some of our long-lost creativity and control, but to have a lot of fun along the way – maybe even raising test scores!

One way to bring these innovations into practice and to help our children get ready for their exciting new world is in a Thinking Classroom. A Thinking Classroom does not threaten existing good teaching, school systems or national requirements, but it does offer an efficient first step on the journey of 21st-century education. By reading this book, you will be given the tools to make your own first steps on this inspiring voyage of discovery. Now it's time to answer the question addressed in Chapter 2.

Chapter 2
What is a Thinking Classroom?

The mind of a teacher should migrate into the minds of the pupils to discover what they know and feel and need.

Horace Mann

Aptness to teach is the power to perceive how well a student understands the subject and to know the next step.

Horace Mann

From Thinking Skills to Thinking Classrooms
Carol McGuinness, DfEE, 1999

On the Art of Teaching
Horace and Mary Mann,
Applewood Books, 1990

www.edwdebono.com

Water Logic
Edward de Bono, Penguin, 1994

This section will:

❍ describe to you the theory behind a Thinking Classroom;

❍ show you one way to put the theory into practice;

❍ develop your own thinking with a thinking tool.

A Thinking Classroom can integrate the finest new teaching methods with the finest traditional practice. Good educators plan, teach and assess. They then use their assessments to plan further teaching. They also attempt to match their teaching to the needs of their students. When discoveries are made about how people learn, when new teaching tools become available and when the world speeds up, a good educator will also look to see how their own practice needs to evolve.

In 1998, when Carol McGuinness was a senior lecturer in the School of Psychology, Queen's University, Belfast, the DfEE (now DfES) commissioned her to evaluate the current research into thinking skills. The result, Research Brief No. 115, *From Thinking Skills to Thinking Classrooms*, is the definitive text for any thinking educator. She summarises thinking frameworks for the classroom, ideas for using ICT and issues of teacher development. She says that good practice is evident, but warns that much more classroom research is needed. She recommends that Thinking Classrooms and the teaching of thinking should have 'a strong theoretical underpinning'.

A Thinking Classroom:

❍ teaches children how to think;

❍ teaches children how to learn;

❍ values and uses the different ways in which children think and learn;

❍ values and uses the different ways in which children are intelligent.

These principles are underpinned by theories of intelligence, learning, thinking and esteem.

You are a thinking teacher (you wouldn't have got this far otherwise). So you may want to challenge some of what you have just read and think it out for yourself. Flowscape is a thinking tool to help you do just that.

Flowscape

Edward de Bono is famous for lateral thinking and powerful thinking tools such as Six Thinking Hats® and Six Action Shoes. He has changed the way the world thinks. One of his lesser known ideas is flowscaping. A flowscape will help you to investigate your thoughts on Thinking Classrooms. A flowscape uses 'water logic'. Water logic is an enrichment of traditional logic, or 'rock logic' as de Bono calls it. Rock logic connects cause and effect. Here's an example:

if John steals Bob's pencil, *then* Bob will punch John; *if* Ann comforts Jane, *then* Jane will feel better.

This is straight-line thinking; the next idea always follows the one before. Water logic is more fluid. It steps back and looks at the different ways in which all the ideas could connect to each other.

Think about what you have read so far. What are your thoughts and questions about Thinking Classrooms? Consider time issues, your current circumstances in school and practicalities. Write down your thoughts below, one next to each letter. Spend a couple of minutes on this. You may be thinking 'This can't work because of other demands.', or 'Where can I find out more?' or 'Where's the evidence?' Whatever comes to mind, write it down.

Then, taking each thought in turn, decide to which of the other thoughts it is most closely related. Thoughts can be repeated. For example, A could be strongly linked to D, and H could also pair with D. Create a list of pairs below.

A	
B	
C	
D	
E	
F	
G	
H	
I	
J	

A		F	
B		G	
C		H	
D		I	
E		J	

Finally, use arrows to join up pairs of thoughts on this diagram. Add an arrowhead pointing to the second letter of each pair.

A   C   F   H

      I   B   J

   D   E   G

Thoughts with two or more incoming arrows are important and can indicate action needed or problems to be solved. Looped pairs of thoughts suggest stability and a final result – your beliefs – which may need challenging.

Your flowscape reveals your response to Thinking Classrooms. You can now create your own principles on which to base your work.

Leave the results for a few days to let the ideas sink into your subconscious. When you return to them, look at the points with two or more arrows. Decide which, if any, of these ideas could form the beliefs upon which you found your Thinking Classroom. 'I'm concerned about getting support to do this.' may not be a useful principle, whereas 'I need to extend my skills as a teacher.' could well be. In this case, the resulting principle could be:

A Thinking Classroom allows a teacher to extend their teaching skills.

You may wish to use my principles on page 7 as they stand. You might want to add, alter, remove or replace some. The choice is yours.

It was only after establishing my four principles that I began to change the teaching and learning in my classroom. This meant that I not only knew what I was doing, but why. Explanation to enthusiastic, interested or even critical others was then straightforward and meaningful. The following section describes what those enthusiastic or critical others had to comment on. As you read the description of life in a Thinking Classroom, can you identify the principles in action?

A thoughtful start

Thirty Year-3 children are lined up outside the classroom. Some are chatting, others look over their spellings, several are preparing to learn – they are performing Brain Gym® exercises (see page 23), guided by posters on the corridor wall. One by one they come into the room. Their teacher sits by the door with her register. She shares a 'Hello', 'Hi' or high-five (hand-to-hand mid-air greeting) with each person. It's a chance to make eye contact and assess moods quickly. Some children have their latest jokes ready, some are upset and a number are bursting with things to tell. Within ten minutes, this thinking teacher has not only registered her class, but has a good idea of what sort of day it's going to be. And the chances are she has headed off many problems.

The children choose one of five activities. They must complete each activity once every week, and think about the order – favourite first or easiest last? They select from a Brain Gym® work-out, a lateral thinking problem, a spelling Mind Map, a thinking book review, and a numeracy challenge. Two children are playing Countdown (the word game) at the computer.

At the whiteboard, children tackling the thinking problem are faced with this: *What can explode slowly, with no smoke or flame?* They write their answers next to the question – an indoor firework, an angry parent, my brother, a big

I like doing Brain Gym®, it makes me focused.
Karen

Dear Tamara,

I've heard that our brains are made of billions of neurons. But I'd like to know how they fit together and what they have got to do with thinking.

Thoughtful, Aberdeen

Dear Thoughtful,

Whoever answers this question correctly will win a Nobel Prize. I will have a go! You are correct; the brain is made up of billions of tiny cells called neurons, approximately 10^{11} in fact (that's 1,000,000,000,000). It is thought that the connections between these neurons total approximately 10^{15}.

Groups of neurons in a particular location (e.g. in the visual processing areas of the brain) can work together to perform a particular function. For example, there are specialised groups of cells at the back of the brain that are dedicated to processing visual information (colour, shape, movement etc.). Electrical signals are sent from one set of neurons to other sets of neurons in order to 'pass on' information; for example passing on the signal that the object seen is a face or a house or that the voice you are hearing is your grandmother's.

It is thought that when a group of neurons fires continuously together they eventually fire in synchrony to reach some critical value which then determines that the signal is passed on. Eventually, information coming from different parts of the brain is integrated (no one is quite sure how this works yet) to create a thought (which might be a memory of your grandmother when you see her face or hear her voice). As a teacher, you might recognise this idea – it's called learning.

Some people have suggested that the frontal parts of the brain are where this integration occurs. It is notable that the brain's frontal part is largest in humans (as compared to apes and other animals) and that this increase in size has helped us to become the unique thinking creatures that we are.

'I'm ready to start work.'

Traffic Lights is good because you wouldn't usually know what you were thinking and feeling.

Karen

red flower. That afternoon, in geography, all answers will be praised for the quality of thinking. All answers are right answers. The whole class will learn that another answer is 'a population', leading to learning about settlements.

After ten minutes, the children assemble by the whiteboard. Their teacher asks them to consider whether they are ready to learn. They show their choice using a three-coloured Traffic Light card (see page 20). Green means ready to learn, red the opposite. Yellow means not sure. The children are learning how to get to green (have a drink, share a worry). Some reds are deferred to a breaktime chat. Over time these children become aware of their moods and take responsibility for their readiness to learn. You could allow a fixed time for this getting-ready activity. It can be used to share ideas – greens help yellows – and should require less time as children gain more skills in becoming ready to learn.

If you are sitting in front of a class of thirty-five children, you may see twenty-five green cards, six yellow and four red. You may know from experience that two of the reds are attention seeking and most of the yellows are thinking about last night's TV. This can be dealt with in various ways – for example deep breathing; a quick song or a visualisation. The other two reds may have serious issues that are playing on their minds. Maybe something is going on at home and they are making a cry for help; maybe there's some bullying in school. You

Song:
Musical and linguistic,
Existential, naturalist,
Inter-intrapersonal,
Visual, mathematical,
Or is it bodily, Which
ones are right for me?

can help by letting these children know that you are aware of their feelings. This can ease the burden on young shoulders. Let them know that you are willing to speak with them after the lesson.

Remember to conduct meetings such as this with an open door and a colleague present. If you have any concerns or if serious issues arise, speak to your headteacher or your school's nominated child protection officer.

By now, the vast majority are focused on learning. They end this getting-ready to-learn session with a song. To the tune of the alphabet song they sing a short piece, with actions, that includes each of Gardner's multiple intelligences (see page 37). The children are challenged to look out for the intelligences throughout the day. As the singing fades, it is time to set to work.

A thinking Literacy Hour

Ask Tamara

Dear Tamara,

Last week, during a Literacy Hour shared text, all of my class fell asleep. When questioned, their excuse was staying up to watch *Big Brother* the previous night. Can you tell me why their brains need to sleep?

Enquiring, Norwich

Dear Enquiring,

We don't fully understand the importance of sleep. What we do know is that sleep is a building process and serves to restore the body's energy supplies that have been used up during the day. Repair work and growth (in the muscle tissue) also occur during sleep. Important hormones (such as growth hormones) and chemicals in the brain are also manufactured while we sleep. The amount of sleep required each night varies but on average it is about eight hours for a human adult and more for a child.

When we don't get enough sleep there can be several types of consequences. Those we can see and experience include a decline in concentration, an inability to focus on the task at hand and losing motor co-ordination. Inside the body, lack of sleep can affect the immune system, leaving us prone to illness. In the brain, some experts believe, sleep gives our neurons a chance to shut down and repair themselves; rebuilding energy stores and dealing with the polluting by-products of cellular activity.

It has also been suggested that during sleep, the parts of the brain that control emotions, decision-making processes and social interactions are less active. This may mean that sleep helps us to maintain optimal emotional and social functioning while awake by allowing these areas to rest. The activity seen in the brain during REM (Rapid Eye Movement) sleep, when we are dreaming, may in contrast be opening up new and different pathways in the brain that are not normally used. REM sleep makes up about 25 per cent of sleep time and occurs every ninety minutes or so. During these times, the brain is very active, dreaming occurs and the eyes move quickly behind their lids.

Earthways, Earthwise:
Poems on Conservation
Judith Nicholls (ed.), OUP, 1993

When we do shared text my arms get achey.

Sarah

Using our different intelligences is good because you know how you learn.

Anina

The text focus today is rhyming poetry. 'My future' by David Harmer is projected onto the wall. The poem considers the future Earth we are making for our children. The teacher wants to use as many intelligences (page 37) as possible. She wants to get every child engaged. She models the reading, drawing attention to rhyme and punctuation. Then the children read it together. The overhead has a green and blue Earth-like tint, and music to support the meaning is playing – 'Lo light' from Peter Gabriel's *OVO*. Linguistic, visual and musical intelligences have already been awakened. The poem asks deep questions about existence and presents images of nature (existential, naturalistic intelligences). The teacher wants to look at intonation and draws on the bodily kinaesthetic intelligence. The children move their hands up and down with the tone of their voices. Then they are asked to choose their favourite phrase and justify their choice to the child next to them (interpersonal intelligence). Finally, they perform a line count and look for the rhyming pattern (mathematical intelligence).

The link into word work is a focus on long vowel sounds. The class is working on ways of making *long a*. The teacher begins a Mind Map on the whiteboard using coloured pens. The children find several ways of making *long a*, a few examples for each, and consider exceptions to the rules.

Word work leads directly into group work. They work at different intelligence areas in the classroom. Some work alone to extend the Mind Map; others work as a team using a flipchart and dictionaries, their task to collect as many *long a* words as they can; several children make words with plasticine. and another group is using visualisation in guided reading with the teacher. As the text is read slowly, the children, with eyes closed, are guided to imagine the characters, actions, scenes or ideas presented.

For plenary, a group that has worked musically performs a song, helped by the classroom assistant. It includes eight *long a* words and has a strong rhythm.

The day progresses. Numeracy, geography and spellings are all delivered in a way which values and uses each child's unique thinking and learning.

With the knowledge you have gained in this section, you are now ready to learn how to create a Thinking Classroom.

Chapter 3
How to create a Thinking Classroom

This section will:

- ask you five questions about your plans to create a Thinking Classroom;
- show you how to make a thinking environment (resources included);
- give you five quick and easy ways to encourage your pupils to think;
- describe how two UK schools have begun to develop their thinking.

Ask Tamara

Dear Tamara,

I recently asked my pupils what they eat for breakfast. Over 70 per cent either had nothing or had eaten only crisps and sweets that morning. I'm sure this is affecting their brains. How? And what should they be eating?

Nutritious, Durham

Dear Nutritious,

Refined sugars, those that are found in crisps and sweets, make blood sugar levels increase dramatically for a short period and then drop dramatically to a level that is usually below baseline. These types of sugars are what cause, in some children, bursts of hyperactivity followed by tiredness. They are not optimum for performance in the classroom. Foods containing carbohydrates (such as pasta, breads and cereal) are preferable. These are slow releasing and will give the child energy throughout the day. It should be noted however that some cereals, particularly those geared towards children, do contain quite high levels of refined sugars. Parents should take care to read the labels on the packets.

To maintain optimum blood sugar levels for the brain to function, lots of small snacks during the day can help. Raisins can be bought in small boxes which can be refilled from a large bag. Small plastic containers can also be used. In the classroom, manage these energy snacks in the way you do the pencils – free, responsible, independent access? Or regulated use? Like any class system, it will depend on the children.

Getting underway

There are five questions about the practicalities that you should now ask yourself. You have already established your principles. By quickly answering these questions, you will create a plan for moving forward.

1. Why?

For a thinking teacher, there's always more to do, there's always a better way. What is your motivation to develop a Thinking Classroom?

- I want to teach the 'whole child'.
- I want to gather evidence on new approaches.
- I am curious about thinking skills and brain-based teaching.
- I am following school policy/action plans.

○ I want to support my special needs children.

○ I want to stretch my able children.

○ I want to try something different.

○ I want to make a difference for all my children.

○ I want to improve my results.

○ Other reasons.

2. Who?

This is not you, but those around you. It is helpful to know who is supporting your endeavours:

○ fellow teacher;

○ year team;

○ year leader;

○ special needs co-ordinator;

○ able child co-ordinator;

○ deputy headteacher;

○ headteacher;

○ specialist teacher;

○ INSET leader;

○ LEA adviser;

○ DfES employee;

○ BPRS (Best Practice Research Scholarship)/college/university tutor;

○ EAZ (Education Action Zone) co-ordinator;

○ other people.

3. What?

There are lots of great places to start; you will find many in the following pages. But once you've decided on it, make sure you understand your chosen idea. How will you do this?

○ Read a book/article.

○ Research on the internet.

○ Watch it in practice.

○ Discuss your plans with a colleague.

○ Present it at a staff meeting.

○ Seek out and attend training.

○ Other ways.

4. When?

Time and duration will give structure to your creative work. When do you plan to begin? Will it be tomorrow, next week, next term or next year – or when you have finished this book? And for how long will you trial your ideas? The possibilities range from one lesson to a whole term or more. You need to decide.

5. How?

You can begin in many different ways. Think about these issues:

○ Explaining your ideas to your pupils – in a special lesson.

○ Explaining your ideas to parents – at a parents' evening or by letter.

○ Setting up a mini-action research project.

○ Starting with a high impact, motivating lesson.

○ Devoting classroom display space to your ideas.

○ Other ways.

Prove it, you've got a year!

Headteacher

What you're trying is a great, calculated risk – go for it!

LEA adviser

Getting ready is the secret of success.

Henry Ford

Your thinking should now be clearer through answering these questions. You will have gained further ideas about what you want to do and how.

Thinking teachers

You will have noticed that this book challenges you to think for yourself, and to create your own teaching. The statements below help to portray a thinking teacher. Note the ones that describe you. You will realise that you are already on the way to becoming a thinking teacher, and may discover some new areas to explore.

- ❍ I reflect on my teaching and seek to improve it.
- ❍ I use the word 'think' and its derivatives often in my class talk.
- ❍ I question what I'm asked to do, looking for reasons/more effective ways.
- ❍ I am prepared to take professional risks to improve my teaching.
- ❍ I value action research as a way to improve my teaching.
- ❍ I am very interested in how my pupils learn.
- ❍ I often ask my pupils what they think.
- ❍ My lessons often challenge pupils to do things like sort, compare, generate ideas, solve problems, make decisions, think of alternatives, reflect, plan, predict and prioritise.
- ❍ I am always looking for better, more effective ways to teach.
- ❍ I don't shrivel up when someone says 'brain' or 'pre-frontal cortex'.
- ❍ I believe that all children are valuable for their unique strengths.

You can model thinking for your pupils through your language, actions and attitudes. By your providing many varied chances for them to think, they will develop a range of thinking skills.

Thinking assistants

When I first decided to set up a Thinking Classroom, I was working with Lisa — the world's greatest teaching assistant. If you have one of those, you'll know how valuable their support is. Teaching assistants are uniquely placed to help a Thinking Classroom to succeed. They often work one to one or in small groups, so they can find out quickly how children learn and what they are thinking. The activity on how children work and learn in the photocopiable resources can be carried out by your assistant and is one of the most valuable tools in establishing a child's learning style.

Simply having another adult in the classroom is an advantage. With a little preparation, you and your assistant can demonstrate thinking and learning through your conversations, like the example on the left (T is the teacher, TA is the assistant).

Assistants can help a thinking classroom develop by:

- ❍ gathering anecdotal evidence about thinking and learning;
- ❍ sharing their own learning and thinking;
- ❍ modelling thinking and learning with you;
- ❍ sharing your principles. (Why not involve them at this stage?)

T: Hmm how is the lesson going?
TA: I'm not sure, what do you think?
T: Well, most of them seem to be learning, but I'm a bit concerned that some haven't understood the task.
TA: I see, what shall we do about that?
T: How about Traffic Light cards?

'I grew some new neural pathways at school today'

Thinking parents

It is always good to have parents on your side. The more opportunities they have to become involved, the more valued they will feel. As you set up your Thinking Classroom, inform parents and offer them opportunities to take part:

- Assess parents' learning styles using the activity mentioned on page 15 – get them to compare their results with their children's.

- Set general thinking homework – e.g. lateral thinking problems, puzzles, brain teasers.

- Set specific thinking homework, targeting one thinking skill – e.g. comparing or predicting.

- Invite parents to a specific lesson to 'help with the thinking'.

- Ask children to teach thinking and learning skills to adult family members.

- Invite parents and their children to a special after-school meeting and set thinking challenges.

Ask Tamara

Dear Tamara,

I read recently that we all have three brains. But I've read somewhere else that we only have one brain split into left and right halves. Which one is correct?

Confused, Essex

copy this

Dear Confused,

I sometimes wish I did have three brains! What you might have read about is notions relating to how the human brain has evolved.

Through evolution we have acquired three components to our brains:
1. The primitive reptilian brain (*archipallium*). This is the oldest part of the brain. It's found really deep, right inside your skull at the top of your spinal column and is responsible mainly for self-preservation.
2. The old mammalian brain (*paleopallium*), which comprises the structures of the limbic or emotional system.
3. Lastly, we have the new mammalian brain (*neopallium*), also known as the superior or rational brain. This includes the cortex which makes up the bulk of your brain mass. It is this part of the brain that does most of the thinking.

In terms of understanding brain function, these distinctions are rarely used in modern neuroscience. Rather, one way of describing the brain is, as you rightly point out, by looking at its two halves.

The brain is split into two lobes or hemispheres, the left and the right. The hemispheres are connected by thick fibres that run through the mid-section of the head, and allow information (in the form of electrical signals) to pass from the left to the right side (and right to left). Some tasks, such as those requiring language, are processed predominantly in the left hemisphere. Other tasks, such as those requiring spatial abilities (knowing where you are in relation to other objects or people), are processed in the right hemisphere. The fibres connecting the two hemispheres allow information from different tasks to be integrated across the brain.

Although there are different areas in different hemispheres of the brain specialising in different abilities, the brain is remarkably plastic and can often find other routes to process information – for example in cases of brain damage, where an ability can recover despite damage to the brain. Blind people reading Braille (by touch) use the same part of the brain as seeing people use when reading words.

○ Invite parents into school as thinking specialists – to explain how they use thinking during their working day.

Involving parents can have very positive outcomes. After running a Thinking Classroom for one year, an end-of-year evaluation revealed the following:

○ Five out of thirty-five parents had independently used some Thinking Classroom ideas in their own work.

○ Twenty-eight out of thirty-five families spoke about Thinking Classroom ideas at least once a week, sometimes daily.

Thinking rooms

Our surroundings influence how we feel and how we act. Not only does a classroom environment affect how children and teachers feel, it can be a great support to learning through display and resources available. Your classroom environment must support thinking. Here are some suggestions.

Ask Tamara

Dear Tamara,

The headteacher in our school has decided that all the children must have water bottles on their desks. She says this will improve their learning. Is this true, and why do my children keep asking to go to the toilet?

Soaked, Manchester

Dear Soaked,

Part of the brain's job is to monitor the internal systems of the body, such as the liver, kidneys and so on. If a child (or indeed anybody) is dehydrated, then part of the brain's activity will be monitoring the water levels in the various organs and alerting them to the fact that they are thirsty. Because of this, brain resources that could be dedicated to thinking are used to monitor the internal organs and alert them to the fact that they need to drink. Dehydration can also lead to headaches (most obvious in the case of being hung over – in adults) which can lead to a disruption in concentration.

An unfortunate side effect of drinking water of course is that children may need to go to the toilet more often. By sipping water rather than gulping it all down in one go, this need may be reduced. There is also probably a 'sheep' effect in the classroom, whereby as soon as one child needs to go, they all need to go. Individual teachers may have ideas about how best to cope with this!

One way to manage toilet visits in a Thinking Classroom is to have toilet tags. These are laminated cards which hang in the classroom. As a child leaves the room to visit the toilet, they take a card, replacing it on their return. Limiting this to two or three cards works well and gives you and the children a quick check on who is where.

A few quick facts:
○ The human body requires up to 2 litres of water per day in order to be properly hydrated. Some of this will come from food. It is recommended that you drink eight glasses of water a day.

○ Thirst is often mistaken for hunger – if a child thinks they are hungry, they should drink some water and see how they feel then.

○ Drinks such as tea and coffee contain chemicals that reduce the amount of water in the body. This may also happen with some fizzy drinks.

Introducing Mind and Brain
Angus Gellatly and Oscar Zarate,
Icon Books, 1999

Mapping the Mind
Rita Carter, Phoenix, 2000

www.funny.com
www.kidsjokes.co.uk

Kids' Silliest Jokes
Jacqueline Horsefall, Sterling Juvenile
Books, 2002

Display
Thinking boards
Divide part of your display area into a grid – one named space for each pupil. In each child's area display their photo or self-portrait; information on their learning, working and thinking styles; a piece of work chosen by the child (with justification); and some of their thoughts/quotations. Every half-term, have the children change their chosen piece of work, and update learning information.

Brain board
You can raise the profile of thinking in your classroom by devoting some display space to the brain – what it looks like, what its different parts do, how it works and how to care for it. At a pinch this can be squeezed into parts of National Curriculum and QCA Science. The 'Ask Tamara' letters will get you started. If you'd like to know more about the brain, try the two books on the left.

Joke board
The emotional reaction to 'getting a joke' is similar to the 'getting it' of learning. This feeling should be cherished, sought after and valued. You can draw attention to it, and bring some fun into the classroom, by setting aside space for the children's jokes – written, illustrated and of course vetted.

Posters
Posters about thinking and learning can be used to teach, review and recall important Thinking Classroom ideas. Either buy or make your own to publicise what you believe to be important in your classroom.

Furniture
Children
There are many ways to arrange the tables, seating and resources. Different seating arrangements are suited to different activities. You can train your children to change rows into a horse-shoe, or groupings of 4 into 8. Think about new arrangements and how they could help thinking and learning. Ask the children to think about which seating arrangements are best for which activities.

You
Your position in the room says a great deal about your teaching style and how you think. Is your desk in the centre of the room, against a wall, or in the caretaker's cupboard? I have tried many approaches to suit different groups. Some responded to a desk at the front with me surveying activity. With others I put my desk in the store room and set up shop with the children at their tables. This was a powerful symbol that I was a co-worker, co-learner and co-thinker and it allowed me to build up a great deal of trust with them.

Resources
Books
There are lots of books on thinking, learning and teaching for teachers – but hardly any for younger children. If you have a say in the contents of your book

corner, go for books about the brain, puzzle books, books which challenge thinking or break the mould.

www.lagoongames.com

Lagoon Games publish a series of lateral and visual thinking books together with a collection of innovative puzzles and thinking challenges.

Toys

Thinking toys such as Rubik's Cube and Rubik's Snake can be used as bribes, as rewards, for practical demonstrations of thinking skills and as wet play activities to encourage thinking. The websites in the margin will point you towards toys and games that engage children through thinking.

www.educationaltoys.com

Educational Toys is an internet toy company which supplies toys from international manufacturers such as the following.

www.hoberman.com

Hoberman: Try their expanding spheres to support visual thinking and symbolise learning.

www.quercetti.com

Quercetti: Quercetti Marble Runs and 3-D gear kits encourage problem solving, predicting and planning ahead.

www.binaryarts.com

Binary Arts: Rush Hour is a very popular problem-solving game in which the player has to negotiate their way through a traffic jam of small plastic cars. Through repeated play, children will develop strategies to win.

www.handsontoys.com

HandsOnToys: Their Toober and Zoots range of foam construction toy is LEGO with a huge spin – many different soft shapes and tubes to connect in varied ways. It frees young minds to create.

www.londongame.com

The London Game Company: They produce Rapidough – Pictionary with Play-Doh®.

Computers

Choosing software can be tricky. However, there are some great programs to encourage thinking. Try these.

www.learningcompanyschool.com

Use the advanced search feature and type in 'thinking'. This will reveal several pieces of software directly linked to thinking skills. These are produced by an American company whose products can also be purchased through www.amazon.co.uk

www.riverdeep.net

Select 'products' from the River Deep homepage, then choose 'critical thinking'. Many thinking-related products will appear. The Thinkin' Things collections address many areas of thinking.

www.evenmorecontraptions.com

Even More Contraptions: For older children and adults, the Incredible Machine is a challenging and addictive puzzle game involving the on-screen construction of wacky machines to solve problems.

www.sherston.com

Sherston Software supply an update of the classic thinking adventure game The Crystal Rainforest.

The best way to fund these resources is to have your work built into the school improvement plan. That way it's official, public and costed. If a Thinking Classroom does not feature in the plan, you could attempt to purchase through subject budgets – ICT or Numeracy, for example.

Thinking children

My son has just started nursery school. He goes to a fantastic beacon state nursery. Every afternoon he plays, learns and grows under the expert eye and guiding hand of his teacher. He is on task for two full hours and experiences structured freedom and independence. What he wants to learn, and how he wants to learn it, is matched to the environment he's in. Why is this not the experience of many older children in schools today? Neil Postman once said that children come to school as question marks and leave as full stops. What goes wrong? How can a Thinking Classroom preserve those question marks?

If you value and use children's thinking, it will become important to them. Maybe a little wonder, curiosity and imagination can keep shining through. Maybe the thinking and learning skills that a Thinking Classroom offers can be brought to bear on curriculum content.

Here are some starter ideas for bringing children's attention to thinking:

- Ask the question 'What is thinking?'
- Have the children draw their minds thinking.
- Have them draw their minds thinking for different activities.
- Repeat this activity every term – how do the responses change and grow?
- Have them design an 'excellent mind' – do the best thinking in lots of different ways. For example, if you combined the minds of children in the class who excel in different subjects into one mind, what would it look like?
- Encourage use of 'Thinking Classroom language'. At a recent Campaign for Learning conference, it was pointed out that children need to look at the language of learning to develop their learning skills. Likewise, considering the language of thinking can help develop the skills of thinking.
- Encourage different types of thinking (deciding, guessing, ordering etc.).
- Ask questions to stimulate and challenge thinking: What, When, How, Why, Who and What if . . .? (See Bloom's taxonomy, page 30.)

Outlines of five tools for getting children's thinking going follow. If you use one or all of them, explain how they work and what they are for to your children.

Traffic Lights

'Hands up who can tell me . . .' How many times have you said that? I once came across a teacher who amazed an OFSTED team with her ability to engage and interest her pupils. Whenever she asked a question, every hand in the class would shoot up instantly. She later explained: 'It's simple, if they know the answer they put up their left hands; if they don't, they hold up their right!'

Every child is born a genius.
Albert Einstein

www.campaign-for-learning.org.uk

In our Thinking Classroom we have fun solving a problem but in pictures.
Joely

How does this encourage thinking? You will know children who always put their hands up and rarely know the answer – the guessers or attention-seekers. Then there are those who never put up their hands, yet know everything. With this teacher's method, everyone gains the opportunity to respond.

Whole-class question-and-answer sessions can be enriched with Traffic Light cards or Thumbs. The Traffic Light card is a small laminated card split into thirds. One-third is red, one orange and one green. The card can be folded so that one colour is shown at a time. Each child holds a Traffic Light card and shows you an appropriate colour. For example, you could ask, 'Who knows four reasons why the Romans invaded Britain?' Explain that showing the green part would mean: 'I know four or more'; the orange 'I know one, two or three reasons'; and red 'I don't know any yet.' The responses give you a visual summary of where your children think they are with this learning. You could record numbers or just get a feel for the distribution of colours. In the plenary session, you could ask the question again to find out whether the children believe they have progressed. Thumbs works in the same way: up, horizontal or down replaces the three traffic light colours.

This is one of the easiest and most effective thinking tools, and there are many ways to apply it.

Question	Responses
Are you ready to learn?	*Green*: Yes. *Orange*: Nearly. *Red*: Not yet. Work can be done with your children deciding on how to get ready to learn.
Have you met the learning objective?	*Green*: Yes, what's next? *Orange*: Nearly. *Red*: I need more time on this.
How can we tidy the classroom quickly, ready for playtime?	*Green*: I'll do the floor. *Orange*: I'm already tidying something else. *Red*: I'll collect the books.
Who has an answer to my question?	*Green*: I do. *Orange*: I'm still thinking. *Red*: I need some help with the question.
What can we do about Samur and David's fight?	*Green*: Send them to the headteacher. *Orange*: Ask them to apologise. *Red:* Let them choose each other's punishment.

Traffic Lights offer a subtle way to enrich your questioning. As there are three possible answers, you have the chance to use open rather than closed questions.

If you decide to make Traffic Light cards, here's a time-saving tip. Slice A4 red, orange and green paper lengthways into thirds, then place a red, an orange and a green strip next to each other inside a laminated pouch, with tiny gaps between. Send it through the laminator and when it's cool slice it widthways into five or six equal pieces. The tiny gaps between colours make folding easy.

Design your own simple notes and photocopy on coloured paper.

Pennies do not come from heaven. They are earned here on Earth.
Baroness Thatcher

Thinking and learning money

Have you ever had a child mutter or even howl the words: 'You can't tell me what to do, my dad pays your wages!'? I hope not – I haven't – but urban teaching myth records such incidents.

To pre-empt such outbursts, get in there first and pay your children for learning. This idea will help create a thinking ethos. You can use it as you wish. You may agree with the principle of financial reward, or you may oppose it – at least, you will have thought about it.

Thinking and learning money can run alongside other reward systems, and it is not limited to academic or behavioural achievements. Your own system could include the use of the money to purchase small objects – pencils, pens, school publicity items and so on. You could have a weekly focus on a thinking or learning skill and an agreed reward. An example is decision making. Your children could be paid each time they make a quality decision. This could be an academic decision – how to present scientific data; or a social one – opting to cheer someone up rather than play football.

Thinking and learning money draws attention to the skills and attitudes which a Thinking Classroom values in a way to which some children can relate. Even the most challenging children are respectful of thinking money – I have never encountered theft or forgery. The only problem has been ownership, which is easily managed by having the children sign the back of each note they receive.

It is a good idea to set a range of prices. This challenges children's thinking: 'Shall I buy a pencil now for 50p or save up for that notebook at £3?' The material reward items can be funded though the school improvement plan. The money can be combined with your existing systems. It can be traded for stickers, behaviour points or free-choice time.

There is a view that reward systems such as this may demotivate children – they begin to focus on the reward and not the feelings associated with new learning. Decide for yourself.

Positive mental attitude (PMA)

Zac Worrall is a teacher with a gift for engaging children. He uses his background in sport to challenge their attitudes and thinking. A positive mental attitude is the prerequisite of any successful sportsperson, and Zac has infused this thinking into all aspects of his teaching. All schools want their children to reach their potential and aspire to great things. Zac has set up a system firmly rooted in sports psychology which helps them get there.

His children are shown how to think positively and to develop confidence in the face of setbacks. He holds up children who succeed against the odds as exemplars of PMA and has developed a system of stickers, rewards and certificates to embed his methods. He models PMA himself by the way he deals with problems in front of the children. It doesn't mean that Zac and his children

There is no failure except in no longer trying.
Elbert Hubbard

Smart Moves
Carla Hannaford,
Great Ocean Publishers, 1995

www.braingym.org.uk

Brain Gym® Teacher's Edition
Paul Dennison PhD,
Edu-Kinesthetics Inc., 1994

are happy and bouncy regardless. What it does mean is that they know how to tackle problems and don't give up at the first failure.

His ideas are so potent that parents have shown great interest and have asked for a similar system for home use. With PMA 'homebase', the attitudes required in his class must also appear in the home. Parents are taught about PMA and shown how it can work. They are given stickers and certificates and shown how to reward PMA behaviour. Communication between home and school targets the cultivation of positive attitudes rather than the punishment of negative ones.

Often we expect our pupils to be ready to learn and to face difficulties with strength and resolve. If you reflect on your own experience, you will see that this may not always happen. How do you react when asked to do something you don't believe you can do? If a Thinking Classroom values and uses thinking, it must develop attitudes which allow thinking to happen. PMA can do this by clearing away negative thoughts, making space for learning. You could decide with your children what a PMA is, how it could be shown in school and ways of rewarding positive thinking and behaviour.

Brain Gym®

If you want to keep your body fit – visit the gym. If you want to do the same with your brain, take up Brain Gym®. Otherwise known as edu-kinaesthetics, this is a series of body movements which can energise and prepare the brain for different learning. Under qualified training, Brain Gym® can also help with some learning disorders.

There are many different Brain Gym® exercises to develop thinking and learning skills and an army of qualified trainers across the UK to help you learn them. For example, cross-crawls are actions with opposites. They stimulate both halves of the brain – preventing reliance on a favoured side. There are many cross-crawl activities – try raising left leg with right arm, followed by right leg and left arm. Repeat this several times. Next, touch opposite elbow to knee, repeating as before. This and other exercises can be worked into the routines of a Thinking Classroom. You may choose to share the theories behind Brain Gym® with your learners, and ultimately children may choose to use selected moves independently to address their unique learning needs. There is an excellent text to get you started. It can be ordered online at www.braingym.org or www.braingym.org.uk

Music

There are many ways to bring music into a Thinking Classroom:

- Setting and changing the mood – calming down/energising.
- Task timing – playing short pieces of music to accompany tidy-up or learning times.
- Supporting subject content – selecting pieces that refer to what is being learned.
- Learning subject content – composing relevant songs and pieces.

Thinking schools

If your drive towards a Thinking Classroom is embedded in paperwork – school improvement plan, action plan, OFSTED action plan, LEA initiative, school policy document, whatever – all the better. And if the whole school is headed the same way – superb! But what about the practical side of making it happen?

www.alns-sec.portsmouth.sch.uk

Admiral Lord Nelson Secondary School decided to have a taster day to get them started – see what happened in the case study below.

Case study

Dare to dream. Aim to achieve.

I am a guest at the Admiral Lord Nelson Secondary School in Portsmouth, for their Thinking Skills training day. Di Smith, charismatic captain, is giving the crew of 70 today's course settings. She lists a string of eminent speakers and workshop leaders from past INSET and celebrates the schools 'challenging and exciting curriculum'. Di was able to handpick passionate specialists for her new school. Over time she has added management expertise and has enriched teaching and learning through innovation. Results are excellent. The school is now ready to refocus effort on classroom practice.

She skims over accelerated learning, and then cites the use of multiple intelligences (see page 37) theory as their next aim. Since 1997 this aspect of learning has been present in the school's study skills unit. Now it's time to develop and embed the practice. She winds up with a tape of Robbie Williams. His poem warns the teachers of the effect words can have on life success.

Now it's over to Nys Abidaon, maths specialist and teaching and learning co-ordinator. As you would expect, the day is well organised. But Nys has a tough job. There is so much to share with the staff, so many new methods which could each impact immediately on the quality of teaching. Each idea could fill a day on its own, but Nys's approach is simple and straightforward. She has picked six ideas and carouselled them into a taster morning. Six 20-minute sessions, run by staff, for groups of 12.

I join a friendly group including linguists and artists and head off to the first workshop. In a cold, bright dance studio, we are introduced to Edward de Bono's Six Thinking Hats® (see page 28) and challenged to create a dance routine. Every two minutes we switch hats, and by the end of the session we have attacked the problem from six valuable directions. The application to creating other products (e.g. artwork, narrative) is immediately obvious.

Along the corridor, in an English classroom, we are presented with a sheet of dots. The task is to find three hidden shapes from their corner points. Some thrive on the task and are quickly halfway through the challenge. Others (myself included) falter and need a strategy. Looking at the next guy's paper works for a while, but it's not satisfying. Eventually we learn methods and feel the 'yeeess!' of learning to do something new. This session succeeded in reminding us of the frustration of not being able to do something, followed by the joy of 'cracking it' – all in the space of twenty minutes.

After a short break for coffee, we have two sessions of co-operative learning. One uses a 'jigsaw' activity to teach different ways of working together. 'Experts' from our smaller groups of 4 come together, learn, and then go back to their original groups to share the learning. In the next activity, we take on roles and play out a scenario of urban regeneration in the Bronx. These sessions show how real group work brings out the need to think and use thinking skills – making decisions, judging, classifying and comparing.

Next, in a modern languages classroom we are given six cards. The words on them are 'analysing', 'synthesising', 'evaluating' and more. We are tasked to place each level of thinking in its hierarchical order. This is Bloom's taxonomy (see page 30). 'Evaluating' draws out the most discussion, and I suddenly realise that we are thinking about thinking about thinking! We match definitions to each level of thinking, then consider how this could be applied in the classroom.

The final session makes a perfect end to the morning. In a science room with wooden stools and Bunsen burners, we learn the ins and outs of learning styles (see page 26). Do learners prefer warm or cold, light or dark, sitting or lying down? How are they motivated and do they learn by seeing, hearing or doing? And did you know that 11–14-year-olds learn best between the hours of 12 and 2 (p.m.)? This session puts the whole morning in context – if we want our pupils to dare to dream, and aim to achieve, we have to value their individuality and develop the teaching that they need.

The school's approach in this case study can be scaled down for smaller organisations and used just as effectively in other key stages.

Thinking about growing, caring and learning

Goldsmith Infant School in Portsmouth has a deeply embedded ethos: growing, caring, learning – hand in hand. It is described by parents as 'a village school in the heart of the city'.

Headteacher Debbie Anderson cares passionately about the growth and learning of everyone in her school. She thinks whole-child, and values the unique strengths and potential in every learner. She lives the message that 'differences are valuable'. In recent years she has embraced national strategies and welcomed their infusion of pace, structure, content and expectation. But more recently she has been thinking a little further . . .

She and her staff noticed that for all their benefits, the strategies were not meeting the needs of all children. Debbie wanted to do something about this, on her own terms. She wanted to seek out and trial some learning and thinking tools which would help all aspects of all children and plug the gaps. It was important that this happened 'in our own way and for our children'.

The school spent a year finding out what could be done. Deputy head Alison Spittles explored multiple intelligences (see page 37), developing an MI baseline assessment and 'intelligent register time'. Others attended Brain Gym® training (see page 23) and learned how certain body exercises can stimulate learning. They also encountered the value of drinking water while learning. Children's attitudes to learning and thoughts about it were investigated using the B/G-Steem method.

Lunchtimes were developed to include a series of activities (dressing up, dance, creative play, quiet time etc.) which involved the children in decision making about their use of leisure time. All these ideas were tried out with an open mind.

Towards the end of the year, the staff gathered for an INSET day of thinking and decision making. Which ideas could be taken forward? Which tools are practical and suitable for our children? How can we value differences and make a difference for each child?

www.surfsouthsea.co.uk/
goldsmithinfantschool

B/G-Steem
Barbara Maines and George Robinson,
Lucky Duck, 1988

A Thinking Classroom is not a blueprint for success or a strategy to be followed to the letter. It is a series of tools based on a simple set of values which you can put to use on your own terms. The teachers of Goldsmith Infant School have picked some ideas that suit their pupils and are learning to use them.

Other ways to kick-start your thinking school are to invite an inspiring presenter to run a day's workshop, or use a series of twilight sessions to explore the ideas. Parents could be informed and involved with a one-off workshop. Individual schools can use Thinking Classroom principles and tools to help create the teaching that their learners need.

You should now be well on the way to a Thinking Classroom and ready to take things further. The next chapter will show you how to develop a Thinking Classroom.

Chapter 4
How to develop a Thinking Classroom

This chapter will:

O introduce you to different ways of working and learning;

O teach you about eleven thinking tools;

O show you how to use eleven thinking tools.

Ask Tamara

Dear Tamara,

A child in my class keeps complaining that his 'brain is full'. Is this possible, and if so, what can I do about it?

Worried, Cumbria

Dear Worried,

It is extremely unlikely that this child has a 'full brain'. What is more likely is that the child has too many thoughts going round in his head and therefore feels that he cannot take on any more information. In order to try to maximise the information the child can take on board, one suggestion would be to make sure that information is compartmentalised into easy 'chunks' or categories.

Secondly, overload can be avoided by changing the mode of input – using touch, sound and sight. For example, do one task that requires him to use the visual domain (looking at shapes or colours). The next task could have the child processing information through the auditory domain – a word-generation task (finding and saying shape and colour words) or listening to a story. In this way, different parts of the brain are being used when the information comes in.

Imagine as an adult what you would be experiencing if your brain were 'full'. You would probably feel that all your thoughts and ideas were whirling round in your head and you couldn't possibly take on any more. I think you teachers call this phenomenon stress. You have probably developed some strategies to try to cope in such situations and children could use these too.

In such a situation, the best thing to do may be to make lists or mind maps of things you really need to have 'online' or in your head at that moment, as opposed to things that can wait. Compress the information through organisation. You could also take a few deep breaths and assess what you need to be dealing with right then. Keep in mind what the first task is, rather than trying to tackle five jobs at once.

Ways to work and learn

It is 6.45 a.m. as I write this. I am sitting at a desk in a warm and dimly lit room. I'm listening to Peter Gabriel's *OVO* album and typing away at my laptop. I've been working for an hour and have taken three short breaks in that time (one for a glass of water, one to practise juggling and the third to put on a Bob the Builder video for my son). This is my preferred style of work.

That's not to say I don't enjoy other ways of working. I love sitting round a table with like-minded people, planning and creating new ideas. That works best in the evening, without music, with diagrams and paper all over the table, and with no breaks apart from refilling coffee cups, wine glasses or water jugs.

As adults, we have probably slipped without knowing into a preferred way of working and learning. We know if we are 'morning people' or whether we can handle interruptions. But what about our children's different styles of working and learning? Is it possible to discover styles and to cater for them?

The secret of education lies in respecting the pupil.
Ralph Waldo Emerson

You may have some flexibility to meet the needs of different styles: lessons can be moved to different times of day; heating and lighting levels can be altered, water and snack breaks can be built into routines, lesson content can be presented in a variety of ways. It would be difficult to cater for every child's style, but offering choices will help them to reflect on how they learn. This could lead them to take more responsibility for their own learning.

Let's consider VAK. This is very popular in schools. VAK summarises three ways in which we take in information: visually (pictures, videos, diagrams); auditorily (words, sounds); and kinaesthetically (movement, touch). As long as sight, hearing or motion is not significantly impaired, learners use all three methods. But each tends towards one. Student testing in the United States by Specific Diagnostic Studies Inc. suggests that roughly a third of students prefer each way. So if teaching is mainly by listening (suiting auditory learners), those who need pictures and movement are disadvantaged.

If you want to know how each child prefers to take in information, look at their eye movement and listen to their words (see Learning style assessment in Photocopiable resources).

The Look–Say–Cover–Write–Check system for spellings is nearly VAK teaching. By thinking about seeing, hearing and doing, this spelling method is enhanced.

Visual	Write words in colour; use bubble writing; make words different sizes; offer line drawings to support word meaning; with eyes closed, imagine the words – make them spin, grow, shrink, change colour, disappear and explode; imagine an image to support the word meaning.
Auditory	Say the word to a partner, whole class say the word (tape it and play it back), say the word in a way that supports its meaning (e.g. say 'small' quietly), sound out phonemes on two or more musical notes; say the word internally (self-talk).
Kinaesthetic	Write the word in the air with a finger or hand (the larger, the better – the bigger the movement, the bigger the memory), write it with both hands/two fingers; stand up to write it in the air; stroll around the classroom with spellings (needs careful management); imagine writing the word in the air, with a sparkler, in sand, in concrete or on a steamed-up window.

As a thinking teacher, you will be aware that children access information in many ways. You can provide for this by giving them something to see, hear and do. You don't need to create any new routines. For spelling, simply slip some of the above activities into your existing spelling system.

VAK is one part of a working and learning style. Little by little, other things can be introduced, for example by allowing a choice of working alone or with others, or by letting children who prefer warmer working to sit nearer to the heater.

You could ask the children to draw what they think their mind looks like when they are thinking, resting, learning and playing. They will begin to realise that there is more to working and learning than sitting still, keeping quiet and copying from the board. You can use the information to make changes to your timetable, classroom organisation or teaching style, or simply to let your children know that you value their differences. However you use the data, by answering the questions the focus is brought sharply onto thinking about learning.

Ways of thinking

There are four ways to bring thinking skills in the classroom:

① *As a separate subject.* A classic, much used example of this is explained in *Top Ten Thinking Tactics*. In a series of ten discrete activities, students learn ten key thinking tactics which can be applied later in other curriculum areas.

② *As a series of skills for a specific subject.* An example of this approach is CASE – Cognitive Acceleration in Science Education. Developed by staff from King's College, London, CASE is a thinking skills programme designed to increase levels of knowledge and understanding in science.

③ *Infused into a specific subject.* This is where a particular subject is targeted, and thinking skills are used to enhance what is already taught.

④ *Infused into all classroom activity.* This is the Thinking Classroom approach, where thinking percolates through all aspects of teaching and learning.

In the following pages you will learn how to infuse what you already do with some powerful thinking tools. Like all tools, pick up and use the ones which suit what you are creating.

Six Thinking Hats®

How does it work?

Edward de Bono has written over sixty books about thinking and thinking skills. One of his most famous ideas is Six Thinking Hats®. It is used daily across the world. The technique uses six different coloured hats, teaching a different type of thinking for each. By thinking in parallel ideas can be created, problems solved and arguments avoided.

As I write, UK firefighters have just ended an eight-day strike. Their horns are still locked with the government over a 40 per cent pay rise and modernisation of working practices. ACAS, the arbitration and conciliation service, is trying in vain to separate them. This is a high-profile public argument. Thinking Hats® could offer an alternative. It presents six different ways to think about the issue, removes egos from the process and focuses on what can be.

As each different coloured hat is placed in turn on the head (metaphorically or even in reality for children) a different thinking style must be used:

Top Ten Thinking Tactics,
Mike Lake and Marjorie Needham,
Questions Publishing,1995

*infuse: to steep,
pervade or instil.*

Six Thinking Hats
Edward de Bono, Penguin, 2000

www.edwdebono.com

White hat	Facts
Red hat	Feelings
Black hat	Problems
Yellow hat	Hopes
Green hat	Ideas
Blue hat	Boss

① White hat thinking is about the facts and the figures. In our example, the 40 per cent rise, the statistic that 250 people a year die in house fires between midnight and 8 a.m. (many fewer die at other times), and the government's aim to reduce the number of firefighters on duty at night are facts. When the white hat is on, it is facts only. Thinking is neutral.

② Facts will bring on strong feelings, and putting on the red hat gives voice to them. This is the emotions and feelings hat and it allows wearers to say how they feel. The pain, anger and frustration of the dispute has a place to be expressed and valued, but is also contained here. Otherwise, the power of the emotions could hijack the whole thinking process.

③ The next hat is black. With this hat on, you think about problems, risks and dangers. You consider what might go wrong. This is negative thinking. In our example, this could be redundancies, fire safety issues and the perils of tinkering with the operations of the fire service.

④ Then we shift into yellow thinking. This is speculative and positive. It looks for benefits and suggestions and allows for dreaming and visions of success. As de Bono says, if the black hat is a glass half empty, then the yellow is 'a glass half full. Of whisky.'

⑤ The fifth hat is green and creative. It breaks out of fixed patterns of thinking to innovate. It seeks to go beyond the known and the obvious to find truly original thoughts and solutions. What if fire-fighters and politicians swapped roles for a week? What if emergency service personnel were given training in each other's fields and money to match — police to fight fires, medics to make arrests, fire-fighters to drive ambulances? And what if some fire-fighters would accept non-cash alternatives — better healthcare and pension rights?

⑥ The final hat is blue. It is the control hat. It thinks about the thinking and decides how the other hats are used. It makes sure that the thinking stays on track and in line with the original issue. With the fire-fighters, it may decide to look at black and white hats first and only move to red and yellow later. Green may not be needed at this time or maybe it could be used first.

How can I use it?

The hats are a powerful and flexible tool. There are many ways to use them, but first, you must set some time aside to tell your children how they work.

'We had a fight'. 'PLEASE can we use the hats?'

I introduced them one day after a particularly hectic playtime. Jake and Amir had let a football disagreement evolve into a full-blown fist fight. Setting aside my own anger and side-stepping the class excitement, I invited both of them to the front of the class and plonked a red hat on Amir's head. I asked him how he felt. I did the same for Jake. We then moved to white hats to establish the facts, and so on until green hats allowed them to create a solution. I managed to structure their calm-down time, and gave them a way to deal with their problem. You may like to consider such opportunities. After a few weeks, with simplified hat names (see above left), the children began to use them for minor disagreements.

Hats are especially useful for:

- ❍ evaluation;
- ❍ comparison;
- ❍ problem solving;
- ❍ designing.

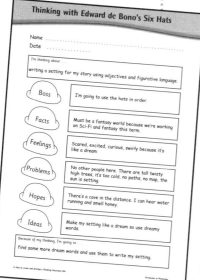

Hats can be used throughout the National Curriculum and therefore in QCA, NLS, NNS and other planning documents. The table on page 31 offers ways to apply the hats in Key Stage 2 for evaluating and comparing. Phrases from the programmes of study are italicised.

There are many applications to problem solving and design in each curriculum area. Rather than drawing up a list, try a different approach. Simply be aware of when your planning requires children to solve problems or design a product (painting, song, poem, graph, spoken presentation, dance, poster, sculpture etc.). At that point, consider if the hats could be used to get the thinking started.

Show me, then!

Here's an example from the National Literacy Strategy, Year 4, Term 2.

Text level work: Fiction and poetry

Reading comprehension	
T3 – to compare and contrast settings across a range of stories; to evaluate, form and justify preferences	Use the hats to think in six different ways about two or more settings. What are the problems in each place? What does each place look, smell and sound like (the facts)? How does the description of setting make you feel? And so on.
T8 – to review a range of stories, identifying, e.g. authors, themes or treatments	The hats can be an alternative book review or reading diary. Each way of thinking can bring out a different aspect of the book. For example: white – an account of events; red – characters' feelings or those created in the reader; green – predicting what could happen next or modifying the story.
Writing composition	
T10 – to develop use of settings in own writing, making use of work on adjectives and figurative language to describe settings effectively	Children may have great difficulty getting started in narrative. Their minds clam up when an original setting is required. The hats provide a template for creating a new place for their story. In the photocopiable resources there is a form that can be filled in for this activity. For an example of how it can be used, see the form in the margin above.

Bloom's taxonomy
How does it work?

Benjamin S. Bloom (1913–99) is remembered as an accomplished teacher, scholar and researcher in the field of education. In 1956, he chaired a committee of college and university examiners. Their task was to discover how students think as they are learning and to classify the different levels of thinking which they found. The result was Bloom's legacy to the world of Thinking Classrooms – Bloom's taxonomy (taxonomy is classification).

Let's think about wine. We know what wine tastes like and looks like, how to make the stuff, where it's likely to be found, that it removes inhibitions and that it can play havoc with our emotions and thinking when taken in excess. Because

Application to National Curriculum programmes of study

General	Assessment of own and others' work
English	◗ En1 Speaking and listening *1f – evaluate their speech and reflect on how it varies* ◗ En2 Reading *4e – evaluate ideas and themes that broaden perspectives and extend thinking* *5f – evaluate different formats, layouts and presentational devices* ◗ En3 Writing *2f – discuss and evaluate their own and others' writing* *9a – imagine and explore feelings and ideas, focusing on creative uses of language and how to interest the reader*
Mathematics	◗ Ma2 Number *1c – select and use appropriate mathematical equipment* ◗ Ma4 Handling data *1b – approach problems flexibly, including trying alternative approaches to overcome any difficulties*
Science	◗ Sc1 Scientific enquiry, investigative skills *2c – think about what might happen or try things out when deciding what to do, what kind of evidence to collect, and what equipment and materials to use* *2i – make comparisons and identify simple patterns or associations in their own observations and measurements or other data* *2m – review their work and the work of others and describe its significance and limitations*
Design and technology	◗ Evaluating processes and products *3a – reflect on the progress of their work as they design and make, identifying ways they could improve their products*
ICT	◗ Reviewing, modifying and evaluating work as it progresses *4a – review what they and others have done to help them develop their ideas* *4b – describe and talk about the effectiveness of their work with ICT, comparing it with other methods and considering the effect it has on others* *4c – talk about how they could improve future work*
History	◗ Knowledge and understanding of events, people and changes in the past *2c – identify and describe reasons for, and results of, historical events, situations and changes in the periods studied*
Geography	◗ Geographical enquiry and skills *1a – ask geographical questions* *1c – analyse evidence and draw conclusions* *1d – identify and explain different views that people, including themselves, hold about topical geographical issues*
Art and design	◗ Evaluating and developing work *3a – compare ideas, methods and approaches in their own and others' work and say what they think and feel about them*
Music	◗ Responding and reviewing – appraising skills *3a – analyse and compare sounds* *3b – explore and explain their own ideas and feelings about music using movement, dance, expressive language and musical vocabulary*
Physical education	◗ Selecting and applying skills, tactics and compositional ideas *2a – plan, use and adapt strategies, tactics and compositional ideas for individual, pair, small-group and small-team activities* ◗ Evaluating and improving performance *3a – identify what makes a performance effective* *3b – suggest improvements based on this information*
RE	◗ Think about visits to places of worship, religious artefacts, and compare different religious practices
PSHE	◗ Think about social and emotional issues
Citizenship	◗ Think about roles, responsibilities and making choices in society

of this understanding of wine, we realise that it may be a useful accessory where some 'social oil' is needed. We may then consider its long-term health issues, its effects on driving ability or the consequences of taking in too much in too little time – regret, severe headaches, inappropriate emotions and actions. This analysis of a double-edged sword led some innovators to create low-alcohol wine. (The hangovers still remain if consumption is high because they are caused by dehydration rather than too much alcohol.) We know a lot about wine, and we could compare it to beer. Which do people prefer? Does beer have the same effect and the same issues as wine?

The previous paragraph demonstrates Bloom's taxonomy in a way you probably won't wish to use in class. It reveals six different ways to think about wine. But Bloom's taxonomy has many classroom uses. Bloom and his colleagues classified levels of thinking like this.

Level	Which means . . .	Example
Knowledge	Finding out	I know about wine.
Comprehension	Understanding	I can explain wine to you.
Application	Making use of the knowledge	I can use wine.
Analysis	Taking apart what is known	I can consider the issues around wine.
Synthesis	Putting things together in another way	I can create low-alcohol wine.
Evaluation	Judging what happens	I can judge beer against wine.

This is a hierarchy of skills in thinking. Children *know* before they can *apply* before they can *evaluate*. But if there's one danger in an otherwise powerful tool, then it's the danger of labelling and limiting. Just because *synthesis* is a higher skill than *comprehension*, that doesn't mean the opportunity to synthesise should be withheld. It's best not to limit children's thinking by saying they are working at one level. You can expose them to chances to succeed at all levels. In fact, by allowing them to think at all levels, you stand more chance of developing the complexity and richness of their thoughts. Try to see that the taxonomy is a series of opportunities, not a developmental scale.

Here's a summary showing six typical skills for each level of thinking. These skills could be used to guide your planning.

Level of thinking	Typical skills
Knowledge	Remember, name, observe, identify, describe, find
Comprehension	Explain, summarise, interpret, retell, order, relate
Application	Use, apply, solve, choose, change, produce, make
Analysis	Investigate, take apart, examine, distinguish, classify, categorise
Synthesis	Invent, create, combine, hypothesise, plan, imagine
Evaluation	Assess, criticise, value, judge, compare, choose

How can I use it?
Anywhere and everywhere! Here are three categories of use.

○ *Questioning*. Different questions can tap into and arouse different levels of thinking. The poster in the photocopiable resources lists simple questions for each level. Why not enlarge it and stick it on your classroom wall? One glance will remind you how to get right inside their heads – at all levels.

A Taxonomy of Educational Objectives
Benjamin Bloom (ed.), Longman, 1956

www.teachervision.com

○ *Extending.* The classroom experience of many children involves finding out and understanding, then, when they finish before playtime, further finding out or maybe some application. For example, I once asked my class to ask and answer questions about what survived from the Roman settlement of Britain. This objective is taken directly from the QCA History medium-term planning document – Unit 6A, A Roman case study. The task involved a visit to a local Roman palace, reviewing the visit, reading several short extracts from Roman information books, then preparing for a hot-seat questioning activity at the end of a lesson. Reading material was differentiated, but I now realise that thinking was not. As children finished, I extended the learning by asking them to find four more examples of the Roman legacy. This was a quantity extension rather than a quality one.

To extend their thinking, I could have based further questions on the taxonomy.

Existing lesson

Knowledge	Finding out	Review previous work; read extracts
Comprehension	Understanding	Prepare to be questioned about knowledge

Thinking extensions

Application	Making use of the knowledge	If someone visited your kitchen after this morning's rush to get to school, what legacy would your family have left?
Analysis	Taking apart what is known	Do artefacts tell us as much about the Romans as the buildings which have survived? How important is each aspect of the Roman legacy?
Synthesis	Putting things together	What misleading legacy could you leave for future generations about 21st-century life?
Evaluation	Judging what happens	How does the Roman legacy compare to the Viking legacy?

○ *Planning.* Look at National Curriculum programmes of study and level descriptors using Bloom's taxonomy. You can get some insights into the thinking of the people who wrote them. Some of the subject authors appear to have had a copy of the taxonomy next to them as they wrote. Science is a good example; Attainment Target 3 (materials and their properties) is typical: level 1 requires children to *know* and *communicate*; level 2 *identify*, *describe* and *sort*. At level 3 they have to *use their knowledge*, *explain* and *recognise*. To reach level 4 *classifying* and *predicting* are added, then for level 5 they need to *identify a range of contexts* (in which changes take place).

Show me, then!

As you begin to understand Bloom's taxonomy, you'll come up with many wonderful ideas for your Thinking Classroom. Some subjects seem more Bloom friendly than others. Design and technology is a good example.

On the left is an example of how children can use Bloom to think about a design and technology project. The blank sheet in the photocopiable resources can be used as your creativity leads you. When applying Bloom to other subjects, start with your lesson objectives and a copy of the taxonomy alongside. Ask each question and see how creative you can be.

Mind Mapping®

How does it work?

A Mind Map is a wonderfully flexible, dynamic and powerful thinking tool. It can be used in teaching and business and by all ages. To get the most out of Mind Mapping®, consult the definitive text (see left). Before you do, here's a quick taster.

Imagine a small stone dropped into the middle of a still pool of water. It splashes, sinks and leaves circular ripples racing outwards from the centre. Research suggests that our brains respond to experience in the same way. If we hear a piece of music, view a painting, talk to a friend or smell and taste our favourite food, our brains radiate many connections from a central stimulus. The Buzans call this 'radiant thinking' – the concept upon which their Mind Mapping® is based.

Put simply, a Mind Map is a visually rich diagram which mimics the way we think. If good old-fashioned brainstorming is a Fiat Uno, then Mind Mapping® roars by as an Audi TT. It has a central idea, branches radiating out and sub-branches coming away from them. Each branch stands for a key idea. The map can be enhanced with colour, shape, pictures, diagrams and single words. Just as your own thinking is unique, so will your Mind Maps be. Each branch, word, symbol and colour will have a special association for you alone. The map which begins this book (see contents page) shows you all you need to know.

How can I use it?

Mind Mapping® has hundreds of uses. In your hands I'm sure many more will be found. Here are three ways to use it in a Thinking Classroom.

- ❍ *Value added.* This is a simple and powerful way to show progress. It shows how good your teaching is and puts children's progress right in front of their eyes. At the beginning of a new topic, and having trained your class to mind map, have the children map what they already know.

  Let's say you are teaching everyone's favourite: electricity. QCA units of work progress like this:
  - ❍ Year 2 Unit 2F Using electricity
  - ❍ Year 4 Unit 4F Circuits and conductors
  - ❍ Year 6 Unit 6G Changing circuits

  At each stage you can assume some prior knowledge – even from a couple of years back. On day 1, the children draw a spark (or another relevant symbol) in the middle of a blank page. Then they map everything they know about the subject, coming out of the spark. Collect in their maps, use them as an initial assessment and finally hide them away in a safe place.

The Mind Map Book
Tony and Barry Buzan, BBC, 2003

www.buzancentres.com

'I always keep the mind maps in a safe place'.

A few weeks later, as the topic ends, instead of a 20-question test on electricity, ask the children to mind map it for the second time, adding points to their original. Ask the children to compare the before-learning and after-learning aspects. They should notice an increase in quantity and quality of subject knowledge and thinking. They could add new main branches and more sub-branches coming from existing ones. There's the progress, there's the learning, there's the value that you have added to the child, right in front of you and them.

○ *Note taking.* I used to find it difficult to teach children to take notes – probably because no one ever taught me how to do it. A Mind Map is more effective. It adds structure and simplifies the job. It copies the way new information spreads into the brain.

In summary, the children should:

○ prepare to identify the main ideas;

○ experience the information and identify main ideas;

○ begin a Mind Map showing the central idea and main ideas on main branches;

○ experience the information for a second time, adding sub-branches;

○ complete the Mind Map with colour, pictures, symbols.

When I use teaching videos in class I always play them twice, back to back. On the second viewing the children are tasked to take notes. They use a Mind Map which they have started between the videos. After the first look, the children will be able to suggest main branch ideas. During the second viewing, the children fill in sub-branches, adding pictures, colours and symbols later. By mirroring their brain processes on paper, the children should gain greater understanding, more lasting recall and a greater ability to think about what they have just experienced.

This model will work in other situations – maybe hearing an audio recording twice or reading selected text twice.

○ *Planning.* There are certain timeless elements of planning for teaching – objectives, activities, assessment opportunities and resources, to name just four. They can be shuffled about in Word or Excel, but all of them can equally well appear on a Mind Map. We do tend to plan step by step, but we are nevertheless holding all the information at once. It makes sense to model the way our mind works in the way we plan.

Suppose you have one hour to teach your children how to mind map.

I would suspect that your mind suddenly shifted gear. Maybe you had a flash of questions – When? How? With what? Why? – followed by ideas about organising the children, resources they would need, expectations for the hour and thoughts on how to check they had learned. You probably considered children who would need support and those who would want to go further. You would know which children could sabotage the lesson and how to head them off. That's your gift as a teacher. If your head is exploding with ideas, map them immediately.

For short-term planning, the main branches could be:

- timetable;
- objectives;
- support;
- extension;
- resources;
- assessment;
- activities;
- notes;
- groupings.

Sub-branches would take the thinking further. For example, *timetable* covers:

- date and time;
- duration;
- class;
- teacher;
- room.

Show me, then!

The Buzans' book, mentioned earlier, is a must. I also recommend three pieces of Mind Mapping® software. MindManager, MindGenius and Kidspiration® can be downloaded free from the internet for a short trial period. I found thirty days long enough to decide on the usefulness of these products. A series of clicks and you have your very own virtual map. It can be edited, saved for later, printed out or placed in other documents.

www.mindjet.com

www.mindgenius.com

www.inspiration.com

Ask Tamara

Dear Tamara,

During SATs, my children become very anxious. What's going on in their brains, and is there anything I can do about it?

Caring, Swansea

Dear Caring,

Anxiety is caused when there is a disparity between what the brain expects and what is observed. Has this ever happened to you in the classroom? This leads to an ambiguous situation that the brain tries to understand and make sense of, which can be difficult. It may be that the situation is novel, in which case making predictions about what is going to happen can be difficult – leading to the so-called 'fear of the unknown'. Similarly, if there is nothing in either long- or short-term memory about the situation it will be perceived as novel and perhaps even threatening (until understood).

When particular parts of the brain are trying to reconcile predictions and observations and anxiety occurs, certain chemicals in the brain are released in order to make the person more alert and aware. This stems from times in our evolutionary history when it would have been important in such a situation to be ready to fight or flee if there was potential danger. Obviously in such as situation as SATs the individual will neither fight nor flee (hopefully), but the same chemicals will be released in the brain.

One way to try to reduce anxiety therefore might be to make sure that the tests they are about to sit are not novel or scary. Practice sessions with SATs or with similar questions would be one way. Other ways might include having short sets of SATs as a lead-up to a bigger exam, making sure that the children are familiar with the set-up they will be exposed to. Similarly, it may be the actual exam situation that makes them nervous – you might set up some exam-type conditions but let the children do something that is fun – joke SATs – but make them sit quietly and do the exercise under timed conditions.

Ask Tamara

Anxiety can also arise when the child feels pressure or a certain expectation, from the teacher or maybe a parent. Although of course these tests are important, it is best not to build them up too much as this will increase the pressure on the child, who will then become anxious about their performance. If a child is anxious about a test it is important that the child is aware of their own feelings and able to talk about them.

Each child is different but there may be some common signs or some signs that consistently appear in one child in response to a stressful situation. Parents and teachers may be aware of these signs and should make sure that they talk to the child about why they are anxious, trying to reassure them. If children are prone to stress during critical periods, it may be worth instructing them in some techniques such as breathing exercises that they can do to help them calm down, slow down and perform better. Similarly, they may use imagination exercises, such as imagining a favourite memory or toy, for five minutes to reduce anxiety levels.

Intelligence Reframed –
Multiple Intelligences for
the 21st Century
Howard Gardner, Basic Books, 2000

Head First
Tony Buzan, HarperCollins, 2000

Multiple intelligences
How does it work?

Are you intelligent? Are you successful? Is David Beckham as bright as Kylie Minogue? Is Mr Spock as clever as Maeve Binchy? And what about your headteacher, your pupils or your colleagues down the corridor?

Just for a moment, put on hold the belief that intelligent people pass exams, read lots of books, can do maths and have high IQ scores. Howard Gardner's theory of multiple intelligences (MI), developed under strict scientific criteria, so far identifies eight intelligences. For example: bodily intelligence (Beckham) is valued alongside musical (Minogue); logical intelligence (Spock) is thought of as highly as linguistic (Binchy). Everyone has all eight intelligences to some degree. With the right training, anyone can develop any of their dynamic multiple intelligences. We usually excel in two or three areas, but Gardner gives equal value to each one.

There are many other theories of intelligence and other definitions of MI.

Intelligence	Characteristics of the intelligence	Careers using intelligence
Musical/ Rhythmic	Awareness of sounds, melody, rhythm. Ability to sing, keep time, compose.	Musician, singer, record producer, music critic, sound engineer.
Naturalist	Awareness of the natural world. Ability to find differences (in nature).	Botanist, wine taster, zoologist.
Linguistic	Awareness of language. Ability to use words and sounds.	Technical author, politician, administrator
Interpersonal	Awareness/understanding of others. Ability to manage relationships.	Salesperson, trainer, team leader, teacher, counsellor.
Intrapersonal	Awareness/understanding of self. Ability to set and achieve goals.	Leader, coach, salesperson, homemaker.
Visual/spatial	Awareness of visual information. Ability to think in pictures.	Pilot, engineer, graphic artist, architect.
Mathematical/ logical	Awareness of cause and effect. Ability to use logic and find connections.	Accountant, lawyer, systems analyst.
Bodily/ kinaesthetic	Awareness of body. Ability to control (with) body.	Surgeon, athlete, assembler, actor.

'Let's use our bodily intelligences.'

www.aspiroweb.co.uk

Intelligences are fun to learn with.

Lucy

Using our different intelligences is good because you know how you learn.

Saba

How can I use it?

From its development in the early 1980s, educationalists pounced on MI as a powerful and empowering theory. They used it to match teaching styles to learner strengths. It has enormous implications for teaching and learning – including curriculum design, school ethos and values, lesson planning and pupil achievement. I'll pick out a few potent uses.

◖ *Esteem raising.* It took me ten years to understand fully and believe the messages of MI: we all are intelligent, we all have all of the intelligences in a unique pattern, we all can become more intelligent. It started with a throw-away comment by a psychology lecturer during my PGCE year. Many years later I used MI in class, with some exciting results. The most profound was in the raising of self-esteem. There's nothing new in saying that every child is good at something, or that children learn in different ways and prefer to do things they are good at. What's new is a scientific theory and research to support these beliefs.

What's also new is being able to tell children exactly how they are clever and then to display it publicly. A way to develop a detailed, dynamic MI profile is described at www.aspiroweb.co.uk; visit the site and navigate to 'MI profile'.

Enter the answers into the questionnaire on the website. You can print out a basic MI profile and hand it to a child and their parents, showing how they are intelligent – not a report showing how intelligent they are. Read that again – it's a subtle but profound difference. If these profiles are displayed in the classroom, each child has daily, public affirmation of their strengths and their areas to develop.

The profile is only a starting point. Gardner argues that any of the multiple intelligences can grow. The profile will be ever changing. It can be added to as you discover more about your children and as they learn.

◖ *Thinking.* I expect you would like to know your own MI profile? Follow the link www.aspiroweb.co.uk to the online questionnaire which will reveal all. But don't be limited by what you find out. Your profile probably tells you what you already know, and will point out the things that you like to do. It may also indicate your preferred way to teach. If you have a strong interpersonal intelligence, are your children always doing genuine group work? If you are dominantly visual, do they have a diet of videos, photos and diagrams? By reflecting like this, you may realise that other types of learning activity could engage children who have different profiles from your own.

Thinking MI thoughts gives you eight ways to consider an issue. Devise your own Mind Map to help children consider part of the curriculum by using the eight intelligences.

○ *Assessment*. I wonder if you can guess which intelligence we use most when assessing children? Linguistic. Written tests and assessment of written work dominate. If you have a strong linguistic intelligence, you'll probably do very well at school. How can we assess and value those who excel in other areas? Using MI thinking, here are eight alternatives (you'll know of many more).

Intelligence	Example of assessment	Example of recording
Musical	Song or jingle	Audio recording
Linguistic	Written test	Keep in teacher assessment folder
Naturalist	Any classification work (e.g. key)	Photo
Interpersonal	Contribution to group discussion	Post-it notes of contributions
Intrapersonal	Mind Map	Keep in pupil portfolio
Visual	Drawing, diagram or piece of artwork	Photo or video
Mathematical	Flow chart, Venn diagram	Keep in pupil portfolio
Bodily	Dance, drama, role-play, model	Video recording, display/gallery

All of the above could be used in an end-of-topic summary, or in many other instances where a written assessment would normally be used.

Show me, then!
Here's an example of infusing part of a literacy lesson with MI thinking. In Year 5, Term 2, children will encounter traditional stories, myths, legends and fables.

Use MI thinking to enrich shared work. Read texts with your children, modelling pace, intonation, pauses and so on. Listen as they copy you, then draw various text features from your chosen passage. This will lead on to your modelling and supporting writing suggested by what has been read. But you'll know children who find it hard to engage with these activities or who are good at faking their attentiveness. Every child sitting on that mat has one or more intelligence strengths, but only linguistic is being developed. The trick here is to use the other intelligences as alternative routes into learning literacy.

The Story of King Arthur
retold by Robin Lister,
Kingfisher, 1994

I've chosen the story of King Arthur as an example. On page 40 are activities for a week of shared text work addressing the following objectives:
T1 to identify and classify the features of myths, legends and fables
T2 to investigate different versions of the same story in print or on film, identifying similarities and differences; recognise how stories change over time and differences of culture and place that are expressed in stories
S5 to use punctuation effectively to signpost meaning in longer and more complex sentences

You'll see that you don't have to include every intelligence in every part of every lesson. What you can do, though, is to offer all intelligences at some time over a week, and in a variety of situations. Children who are turned on by maths but shut down in literacy, for example, have an opportunity to use what they are good at in a place where they have to improve.

Day	NLS objective	MI activity	
Monday	T1	◗ Read page 5 (Merlin's cave) to children. ◗ Read it with children. ◗ Children read it to you. ◗ Use hand-held recorder to tape children.	◗ Play it back and ask for comments. ◗ Ask pairs to identify genre and at least five key features (of a legend). ◗ Ask pairs to negotiate their most important feature to share with class.
		Intelligences: linguistic, interpersonal, intrapersonal.	
Tuesday	S5	◗ Re-read extract. ◗ Focus on punctuation: use hands signs to indicate different punctuation marks (point with finger for full stop, make C	for a comma, make capital T for new sentence). ◗ Pairs use highlighter pens to mark key features of the story (knights, adventures, magic, monsters etc.).
		Intelligences: linguistic, bodily, visual, interpersonal.	
Wednesday	T2	◗ Show extract from the film *Merlin** set in Merlin's cave. VIDEO REF: *Merlin* (1998), Director Steve Barron, ASIN B00004CYZX, Catalogue Number CC9021	◗ Be aware of music used and features of the forest setting. ◗ Record details of video on a Mind Map. ◗ Homework – find a piece of music which would go well with the soundtrack to *Merlin*.
		Intelligences: linguistic, visual, musical, naturalist.	
Thursday	T1 T2 S5	◗ Show video extract of Arthur pulling the sword from the stone. ◗ Read the equivalent extract from the	book, using punctuation hand signs. ◗ Ask groups of 3 to discuss similarities and differences between video and text.
		Intelligences: linguistic, interpersonal, visual, bodily.	
Friday	T2	◗ Ask groups of 3 to prepare a Venn diagram comparing the previous day's video and text extracts. One child is	responsible for each circle and the third for the overlap and outside area. ◗ Display Venn diagrams. Children assess each other's work.
		Intelligences: mathematical, linguistic, interpersonal, visual.	

* This film contains some scenes not suitable for young children.

www.newcityschool.org

Celebrating Multiple Intelligences: Teaching for Success
Faculty of New City School, 1994

Succeeding with Multiple Intelligences: Teaching Through the Personal Intelligences
Faculty of New City School, 1996

www.networkpress.co.uk

Two of the best books around for MI teaching ideas have been produced by the faculty of New City School, St Louis, Missouri. You can order them direct from the school. Visit their website to do this.

Network Educational Press (NEP) publishes sets of MI posters which reinforce the idea that everyone is intelligent in their own unique way.

Thinking stories
How does it work?
All peoples and cultures use language to think and communicate. Stories carry the ideas and memories which are valuable to those cultures. From the legend of King Arthur to Harry Potter; from the daily TV news to a tale told to a friend in a pub – stories are the trusted guardians of facts, beliefs and values. And everyone has a story to tell.

Stories stimulate thinking. A well-told story will kindle raging fires of thought in your children. With your words and actions you can captivate their minds, engage their thinking and make your thoughts theirs – that is, teach.

How can I use it?

A well-chosen story can deliver curriculum objectives and develop thinking. And a well-delivered story can be a very special experience for your class.

Story telling must be structured. The delivery is important and follow-up questions are needed to draw out discussion and thoughts. Other thinking tools can be employed here – Bloom's taxonomy or Six Thinking Hats®, for example.

The Oxfam Book of Children's Stories: North South East and West
Michael Rosen (ed.),
Walker Books, 1992

○ *Curriculum objectives.* New topics and lessons should begin with an engaging stimulus. There are many ways to get attention – a funny hat, a video, a challenge, a picture, an artefact, a joke, a police officer, a problem, something unexpected, a question or puzzle. A story can do the same job, especially when it captures the learning objective. I'm suggesting you turn what you know about a subject into a story, or find someone who can. For example, QCA History, Unit 18, asks the question: 'What was it like to live here in the past?', and seeks answers through a local study. If you have lived locally, or know the area, there will be stories to tell. Otherwise, a parent, grandparent or older member of the community could recount the war years or the 1970s, or recall how the area has changed in their lifetime.

QCA Geography, Unit 10, looks at a village in India. A flick through the contents page of a multi-cultural story anthology should reveal an appropriate tale. 'The Four Brothers' in *North South East and West* would set the scene for this topic. The questions which follow the story would lead into the required learning objectives.

Stories for Thinking
Robert Fisher, Nash Pollock, 1997

○ *Thinking skills.* Dr Robert Fisher works at the Centre for Research in Teaching Thinking (CRITT) at Brunel University. He has published widely on the theory and the practice of developing children's thinking. In *Stories for Thinking* and his other resources, he presents a wide range of tales, each followed by key questions. He also suggests further activities.

The skills of thinking are many and varied. The skills below can all be brought to bear on a story:
  ○ planning (a new story);
  ○ ordering (the events);
  ○ sorting (types of story, types of event);
  ○ solving problems (which the characters encounter);
  ○ creating ideas (for new stories, for alternative endings);
  ○ deciding (what a character should do next);
  ○ choosing (an alternative path);
  ○ classifying (genre, character);
  ○ comparing (one story with another, characters, events);
  ○ predicting (the outcome, resolution).

www.teachingthinking.net

Show me, then!
Below is an original story told for its own sake. The questions have been worked out by thinking with Bloom's taxonomy and six hats. Maybe you could think about which question comes from which hat and which level of thinking.

The wonderful king and the sweetest fruit

There was once a wonderful king who loved his kingdom and all the people in it. And his love was returned in equal measure by his loyal subjects. However, like all wonderful people, he did have one weakness. The king's weakness was FOOD! Food, food, food. He just couldn't get enough of it. He ate from the moment he woke up until he fell asleep at night. He ate before breakfast, he ate during and after breakfast, he had elevenses (and nineses and tenses). He ate lunch, tea, supper and all the meals he could fit in between. He ate and ate and ate. And he didn't eat any old food. Oh no, only the best was good enough for him. The finest cakes, the crustiest bread, the most tender meat and the sweetest fruit. He always expected the best. However, like all wonderful people, he did have another weakness. His other weakness was that he was never satisfied. He forever wanted a finer cake, crustier bread, more tender meat and above all a sweeter fruit.

One evening, after a particularly tasty (though not quite satisfying) meal, a minstrel came to his court and began to sing. He sang of adventures in far-away lands, of heroes, heroines, monsters and long-lost treasure. And towards the end of his song, just as the king was falling to sleep, he sang of an island where a tree grew, bearing a fruit the taste of which would bring the deepest, sweetest and greatest satisfaction.

The king awoke instantly and demanded to know where the fruit could be found. The minstrel could remember a few more lines, but those only hinted at where the island might be. Nevertheless, the following day the king set off alone on his quest. As if in a dream he wandered far and wide for seven years and seven days and eventually came to the island.

He gasped as he drew near to the tree. Hundreds of skeletons and bodies, all twisted and broken and with their mouths wide open, littered the ground. But the draw of the fruit was great and he stepped over the horrors. There was a ladder by the tree and the king began to climb. Soon he came to the top and there it was – the sweetest fruit. Even the sight of it made the king's mouth water like never before. The smell of it nearly made him fall off the ladder. He reached to take the fruit, but it was too far away. He reached again, further this time, but the fruit seemed no nearer to his hand. He twisted and stretched and wriggled on the ladder, all the time desperate for the fruit, yet terrified of falling. And then it dawned on him why the skeletons had their mouths open – the only way to taste the fruit was to jump from the ladder, grab it, and taste it as he fell to his death.

What was he to do? Jump and eat the fruit, yet not live to tell the tale, or slowly climb down the ladder knowing that for the rest of his life he would be haunted by the memory of the sweetest fruit that he never tasted?

Six hats	Bloom
What did the king do in the story?	What happened in the story?
How did the king feel when he was on the island?	What would you do if you were the king?
What was the king's problem?	Have you ever had a difficult choice to make?
What did the king hope to do?	What made the king act as he did?
How could the king get the fruit and live?	What would the king have done in a different situation?
Which question is the most important?	How do the king's actions shape up compared to our prime minister's?

Thinking Through Geography
Simon Chandler and David Leat,
Chris Kingston Publishing, 2001

Living graphs
How does it work?

The National Curriculum mathematics programme of study, Ma 4 Handling data, presents fourteen statements, each beginning 'Pupils should be taught to'. With careful use, a living graph can address all fourteen and more. It can be applied wherever data are being collected, processed and represented.

A living graph is a simplified graph or table and a series of statements. The statements are loosely linked to the data, but pupils are tasked to find direct connections. This generates discussion, argument and a range of thinking – guessing, justifying, testing, refining ideas and analysing.

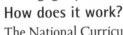

Instead of just counting vehicles that pass the school gates for ten minutes, using coloured pencils to produce a block or bar chart of results and displaying the result, try the living graph exercise in the photocopiable resources. It shows traffic flow over fifteen hours along one street. The two bulges are a.m. and p.m. rush hours.

Each statement about the Woodhouse family can be associated with one or more bar on the graph. For example, fact 6 (Mr Woodhouse wakes up – it's quiet and dark) may be at a time when traffic flow is light and the bars are small. There are three possible places. Children may base their ideas on experience, imagination or both. There is justification for all three places: on the far left as he gets up for work, in the middle if he is unemployed or on shift work and it's a very cloudy day, or on the far right if he's had an early night and woken up for a drink.

Living graphs stimulate thinking and encourage debate. With clear organisation and the freedom to argue about different answers, children will learn not only to interpret graphs but to handle ambiguity.

How can I use it?

Living graphs can be adapted for different ages and used in any subject where data are represented graphically. Three subjects, in addition to mathematics, are obvious choices.

○ *Science.* Much of science can be graphed, so much of science can produce a living graph. A well-constructed living graph can support Sc1 Scientific enquiry, especially PoS i, j, k, l and m – considering evidence and evaluating. It also reinforces knowledge from the other attainment targets. Here are three ideas, one from each attainment target. You'll come up with your own as adaptations to what you already do.

○ *History.* History considers changes over time; so do living graphs. Here are some possibilities linked to National Curriculum study units.

○ *Geography.* Geography encourages thinking and learning about people and places. It asks and answers questions from individual to global levels. Here are some potential uses for a living graph.

Science

Attainment target	Living graph example	Questions focusing on . . .
Sc2: Life and living processes	Changes in population of urban foxes over several years	. . . a family of foxes
Sc3: Materials and their properties	Temperature of coffee in a cup over a few hours	. . . a busy teacher who never gets round to drinking their playtime coffee
Sc4: Physical processes	Length of shadow cast by a stick during a school day	. . . one pupil's activities during school day

History

Study focus	Living graph example	Questions focusing . . .
Local history	Growth of housing over time	. . . a long-established local building firm
British history	Population in an area of England from AD 42 to AD 142	. . . living conditions of three generations of a family
World history	Water level on Nile flood plain over a year	. . . a Nile farmer

Geography

Programme of study	Living graph example	Questions focusing on . . .
5a: recognise how people can improve the environment	Litter on school field/ playground over a year	. . . the planning, organisation and running of a litter-picking team
3f: describe how places are similar or different	Noise level in a city/village over one day	. . . a pop group trying to record a live track out of doors
4b: recognise some physical and human processes	Number of road closures due to flooding over a year	. . . a postal delivery service

Show me, then!

If the data and graph you require are already available, well and good. If not, create a graph which follows the general pattern you want to show. It's a good idea to think of the story that's being told by the graph, then attach statements to specific points. Remove the statements. It's now the children's task to put your thinking back together again. Here is an example:

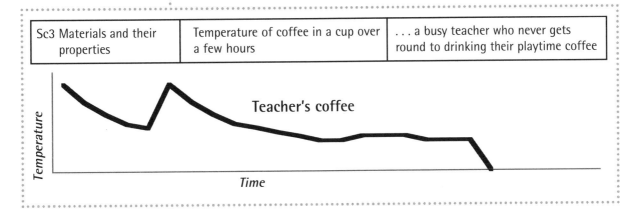

| Sc3 Materials and their properties | Temperature of coffee in a cup over a few hours | . . . a busy teacher who never gets round to drinking their playtime coffee |

We know that coffee will slowly cool in a fairly uniform manner, so I've added a few anomalies: a sharp rise in temperature, a plateau and a drop to zero. The first step is to create the story of events around the cup of coffee.

The coffee is made at playtime, then begins to cool. The teacher is distracted by a new government initiative and leaves his coffee in the staffroom. It continues to cool until he discovers it at lunchtime and pops it in the microwave. Then a fight breaks out in the lunch hall and he is again separated from his caffeine. In the remaining fifteen minutes of lunch he marks spellings and puts the finishing touches to the afternoon's lessons. The forgotten coffee continues to cool, but the afternoon sun has now swung round and is beating down through the staffroom window. The coffee's decline in temperature is arrested and eventually rises slightly. At the end of the day, gasping for a coffee, the teacher passes his teaching assistant in the corridor with a tray of empty cups.

The final step is to pull statements from the story for the children to link to the graph. The statements need to be shuffled to confuse those who would quickly pick up a chronological pattern:

◗ The sun comes out in the afternoon.

◗ Mr X sorts out a fight in the dining room.

◗ Mr X makes a cup of coffee at playtime.

Try creating further statements of your own.

Memory teams

How does it work?

David Leat from the University of Newcastle is a prime mover in the research and application of thinking skills. His focus is geography, and his memory mapping is an excellent tool for making geographical maps from memory.

More Thinking Through Geography
Adam Nichols and David Kinninment, Chris Kingston Publishing, 2001

A memory team is simply an application of a memory map to other subjects and contexts. It's a fun way to get children learning, thinking and thinking about their learning.

A memory team is a group of 2–5 children tasked to reproduce an image, piece of writing or other source of knowledge. Copies of the source are hidden and viewing time is limited. What's more, team members are only allowed to view the source one at a time. Each child must remember as much as possible before returning to the group to reproduce, or pass on, their observations. The next team member has their turn and so on until the copy is made. On completion, the work of the memory team is compared to the original. At this time, the teacher can draw out strategies which were used, and debrief team effectiveness.

Let's take a newspaper article as an example – an illustrated story about the life of a famous artist. It is being used as a stimulus to begin a topic about the artist's work. Three copies of the article are placed on flipchart stands around the room, facing away from the children (depending on copy size and class size, additional copies may be needed).

In groups of 3, the children are given a minute to decide on an order of viewing (A, B, C) and are told they will be copying something hidden on the stand. The A children from each group have twenty seconds to view a copy of the article and return. The group is allowed thirty seconds to discuss the task – maybe deciding on a strategy: 'B, we need another look before we can plan; C, you get the headline and, B, you get the layout.' Next the B children have twenty seconds, followed by thirty seconds of discussion. Finally the same time is given to the Cs. From then on, children have regular 20-second viewing slots in turn until the task is complete.

From experience, the first time is likely to be messy – incomplete work, arguments, sulks, children taking over or sitting out. It's all dependent on pre-existing collaborative skills. That's why the debrief is important. Why not use another thinking tool to plan your debrief?

Debrief questions suggested by Bloom's taxonomy:
- What happened?
- Did every team member take part?
- What are the similarities and differences between the copy and the original?
- Why are there differences?
- What skills did your memory team use?
- What problems were there in your memory team?
- How did the team use its skills?
- How did the problems get in the way of your success?
- Did your team work better or worse than last time? Why?
- What does your team need to do differently next time to succeed?
- Where else do you use these skills?

We do not remember days, we remember moments.

Cesare Pavese

Children who know how to reflect on their own and others' performance will quickly take on board feedback from a debrief like this.

How can I use it?

Memory teams can be used for learning in every subject. Here's a list of ideas. Remember that the source must be kept hidden from all but the current observer. The task is to reproduce it as closely as possible. For audio, a separate area or headphones will be needed.

Mathematics	Graph, frequency table, chart, new multiplication table, multi-link pattern, collection and arrangement on a coordinate grid of 2-D or 3-D shapes
English	Newspaper article, text extract, poem, book selection
Science	Graph, apparatus set-up, selection of equipment, raw data
History	Evidence – artefacts/written/visual, living resource (guest historian answering set questions)
Geography	Maps, graphs, population data, environmental images, countries/capitals and flags
Music	Short repeating musical phrase or soundscape, a rhythm
Art	Piece of work by famous artist, selection of colours, pencil shading intensities, selection of tools and materials
ICT	Software/task instructions, database, spreadsheet, artwork
Design and technology	A construction, e.g. multi-link tower, product requirement, product information
RE	A series of artefacts, a set of photos
PSHE	A selection of medicines (kept out of reach), pictures of social issues (friendship, bullying, family etc.)
Citizenship	Swimming pool rules, charity leaflet, relevant newspaper article
PE	A set of instructions for a game, dance, strategy or gymnastics sequence

You can give team members different roles. A alone could view, and can only talk to B, who has to pass on the information to C, who is the only child allowed to record.

Show me, then!

The arrangement of shapes on the memory team shapes page in the photocopiable resources can be copied by a memory team to learn about shape, position and movement (PoS Ma4 2a, b, c, d and 3a, b, c). You can create different combinations to match the learning you wish to take place.

In this example, one child has a pencil, ruler and piece of squared paper. They are the recorder. The other children take turns to visit the shape grid and pass its details on to the scribe. The activity progresses as described previously.

Neuro-linguistic Programming (NLP)

How does it work?

I can give you only a flavour of NLP here. You'll get a feel for what is possible and see the potential, but be aware that this is a very large subject area.

Frogs into Princes
Richard Bandler and John Grinder.
Eden Groves Editions, 1990

The Elements of NLP
Carol Harris,
Element Books, 1998

Awaken the Giant Within
Anthony Robbins,
Pocket Books, 2001

The mission of NLP is to enable people to get better at what they do by modelling the behaviour of those people who do it well already. This is not hero worship – there's a difference between pretending to be Michael Owen at playtime and identifying and learning his unique skills one by one.

NLP allows people to understand themselves, to consider how they would like to grow and what they are capable of. It then gives them the methods to enable them to change. This has direct relevance to the classroom. We want to know our pupils' abilities and potential and how to help them achieve. And as thinking teachers, we want to share this knowledge with them.

Neuro (relating to the mind and how it works)-linguistic (how we express our experience of the world) programming (habits and patterns in our behaviour) was born in the early 1970s at the University of Santa Cruz, California. It was conceived by two people. The first is Richard Bandler, known as the sponge, who has an extraordinary ability to absorb other people's patterns of behaviour. He had studied maths, computing, physics, psychology and philosophy. The other is Dr John Grinder, known as the chameleon, an assistant professor of linguistics who spoke several languages. These two men used their talents to absorb and analyse the behaviours of many successful people. The result was a set of behaviours that, if copied, could bring others similar success.

Since then, the study and use of NLP has spread. It is used in education, advertising, business, entertainment, retailing – any place where people are. Many leaders, followers and users of NLP have appeared. One is Anthony Robbins. The hypnotist Paul McKenna uses NLP and trains others to do the same.

How can I use it?

NLP already happens in classrooms. Very successful teachers will be doing something different. That difference can be identified, quantified and copied. The same applies to successful pupils. By looking at how they succeed – what they do, feel and think – and copying it, others can make similar achievements.

Of its many uses, here are a couple for the classroom.

◐ *Beliefs about learning.* A belief is an idea which we hold onto and defend. It's usually supported by evidence and can empower or sabotage us in our aims. How often have you heard comments like these in the classroom?

◐ It's too hot to work.	◐ Science is stupid.
◐ I always lose my books.	◐ I'm thick.
◐ I can't do it.	◐ I don't see the point of this.

Robert Dilts worked with Bandler and Grinder. He created the idea of 'neurological levels'. Like six hats and Bloom's taxonomy, it is a framework for thinking. It names six ways in which a person can operate. The disempowering words above can be classified as follows.

Neurological level	Application to learning	Pupil words
Environment	The where and when of learning	It's too hot to work.
Behaviour	Actions, responses and reactions during learning	I always lose my books.
Capability	Knowledge, skills, and strategies for learning	I can't do it.
Belief	Ideas about learning and motivation to learn	Science is stupid.
Identity	Self-knowledge and self-identity as a learner	I'm thick.
Spirituality	Reasons to learn	I don't see the point of this.

This is gold dust for a thinking teacher. It's a window into exactly what is stopping the pupil from learning. If you recognise that a child is stuck at one level, then you can try to unblock them on that same level.

Pupil words	Typical teacher response	Thinking teacher response on same level
It's too hot to work.	Open the window and take off your jumper and coat. And hat and gloves. It's July.	What can you do to make the room cooler?
I always lose my books.	Get a piece of paper.	Who can show you how to keep them safe? What don't you always lose?
I can't do it.	Yes, you can.	What can you do? What parts of it can you do?
Science is stupid.	Back to work, please.	Are other subjects stupid? What makes a subject stupid?
I'm thick.	No, you're not.	How do you know you're thick? What are you good at? (Use multiple intelligences arguments here – see page 37.)
I don't see the point of this.	You don't need to, just do the task.	Can you see a point to anything you do in school? (Be careful with this.)

I know you'll be under time pressure, and the above could lead into some lengthy discussions. But the potential is there to unblock children's learning. It's up to you to decide if that is time well spent.

● *Memory and recall.* By studying how people successfully remember and recall information, we discover a set of tools to help us and our children do the same. NLP teaches us to use imagination and actions to remember things. With our imagination, we can link what we wish to remember to something we already know. We then manipulate the image in our heads — changing its shape and colours, making it move or making it funny or absurd. In addition, a body action gives the brain a body memory to supplement this imagination.

As a quick example, I had trouble remembering the names Bandler and Grinder. The way I cracked this was to say Bandler out loud whilst imagining a huge green rubber band being flicked by a cartoon sponge. Grinder I recall as an old-fashioned hand-turned grinding wheel with a many-coloured chameleon running for its life on top. To add a body memory, I flicked an imaginary rubber band and turned an imaginary handle respectively. This may seem absurd, but I bet you've now learned that Bandler was the sponge! Try it with your class next time there are facts to learn.

Show me, then!

Let's look at spelling and return to VAK (see page 27). Successful learners excel in one or more of these styles: visual, auditory, kinaesthetic. If you can establish a preferred learning style, teaching can be matched to it. It's important, though, not to label and limit. For example, dominant visual learners should have the chance to develop their auditory skills.

Predicates is another NLP tool. It adds evidence to eye accessing cues. When people are thinking visually, they tend to use phrases like: 'I *see* what you mean' and '*Watch* out!' Those who prefer auditory mode go for: 'I *hear* what you're saying' or 'It *sounds* good to me.' Those thinking kinaesthetically may say: 'It *feels* right' and 'That's *cool*!'

The mouths and eyes of your learners can yield gems of useful learning-style information. You can use this in class to set up varied activities tending to each style. Children can either choose the activity, or be moved round each one. For example, in Literacy Hour groupwork focused on using adjectives, provide:

- objects to handle and describe (kinaesthetic);
- pictures/video to watch and take notes from (visual);
- a taped story to collect adjectives from (auditory).

This could take place over three sessions, with children charged to learn in three ways in rotation, or as a longer one-off activity in which children choose how to learn. With your careful and efficient classroom management, they will deepen and broaden their learning ability.

For more information on NLP and its many uses in the classroom, contact the NLP Educational Network. Innersense run courses on the application of NLP in the classroom. You can contact them through their website.

www.new-oceans.co.uk

www.innersense.info

Thinking pictures
How does it work?

The technical name for thinking pictures is metacognitive graphic facilitators. We'll stick with the short version.

A Mind Map is the ultimate thinking picture – a means of representing information which mimics thought. However, there are many other ways for children to record their learning which acknowledge the way their minds work. A flow chart is one example. It illustrates linear, logical thought.

How can I use it?

Whenever you plan for your children to write and record information, be more specific and choose an appropriate thinking picture. Its form can be demonstrated on the board or on a photocopied sheet. As your pupils use a growing range of thinking pictures over time, they will be able to choose which one is suitable for the task in hand.

When children become adept at thinking pictures, they may tend to use only one or two – part of their preferred style. Your response as a thinking teacher can be as follows:

○ Praise, encourage and develop the use of just one or two pictures.

○ Encourage the use of other pictures.

○ Challenge the child to create new pictures.

Show me, then!

The photocopiable resource entitled 'Thinking pictures' offers nine thinking pictures and the following page provides suggestions for their use – one for each National Curriculum subject. Each picture can be applied in many further ways. Remember that there are many more thinking pictures in use, and lots that you can create for yourself.

Odd one out

How does it work?

Who is the odd one out?

① Mother Teresa   ③ The Archbishop of Canterbury
② Adolf Hitler   ④ The Dalai Lama

Odd one out is a very simple and very powerful motivator to think. You probably chose number 2, Adolf Hitler, basing your decision on morality and adherence to the law. Adolf Hitler was not a good and holy person.

However, if we change the criteria, Adolf is no longer the odd one out. If we were looking for males, Mother Teresa would be the nonconformist. Leaders not in exile would exclude the Dalai Lama. The Archbishop won't fit if we're thinking about people without place names in their official titles. (What about Mother Teresa *of Calcutta*, you are wondering. You are thinking and challenging the relationships between these four people.)

The activity challenges children to look for relationships, to look for exceptions and to classify information.

How can I use it?

Start a lesson with an odd one out challenge. Option A used to be my preferred method until a helpful OFSTED inspector pointed out that the children should really be awake for lessons.

Option A: Traditional lesson beginning	Option B: Odd one out lesson beginning
Over the next hour we're going to learn about skeletons	Which is the odd one out? **Horse, Snake, Beetle, Worm.**

'Which one is the odd one out?'

Think about the opportunities of option B. The beetle is the only one with an exoskeleton (skeleton on the outside), the worm is the only one without a skeleton, and the horse is the only one which can damage you with a movement of its skeleton. In each case, three animals have something in common while the fourth is a misfit.

Children have the opportunity to show off their original thinking. Often there is no one correct answer. You'll be amazed by the variety of solutions your pupils give. Each child may pick up on a different relationship between the items in the list. They will have many reasons why each item should be the odd one out. Remember that the remaining things must have some connection to each other.

Show me, then!
To create an odd one out challenge, first think of the learning you want to take place. For example in design and technology, the objective could be *identify the moving parts in a toy*. Think of (or get hold of) two or more toys with moving parts – Barbie doll, toy car, Rubik's Sphere. Then find a toy with no moving parts – a ball, for example. Finally, test each item for 'oddity'. The Barbie doll is the odd one out because the others will roll on a flat surface. You need to use only one hand to play with everything but the Rubik's Sphere.

You can develop this activity with astute questions. What sorts of moving part are there? The car wheels move on their own after a push, but Barbie needs help. How could a moving part be added to a ball to make it a better toy?

An activity sheet in the photocopiable resources offers some odd one outs for different subjects. Try them for yourself, then decide how you could use them. Create your own sets for specific lessons.

Real brainstorming
How does it work?
Most of us brainstorm with our children. But do we brainstorm correctly? Brainstorming is not Mind Mapping®; it is a way to generate new ideas. It can happen individually, or in pairs, or groups, or as a whole class, and it should follow some simple rules:

The best way to have a good idea is to have a lot of ideas.

Linus Pauling

① Understand the problem.
② Choose a scribe.
③ Don't criticise ideas.
④ Don't praise ideas.

⑤ Get as many ideas as possible.
⑥ Be wacky.
⑦ Set a time limit.
⑧ Only evaluate ideas afterwards.

In a good brainstorming session, ideas bounce around the room like fireworks. One child's thoughts trigger another's, whose idea helps someone else remember something useful. This can happen because the children are allowed to be wacky and do not get hijacked by the emotions of getting it wrong (rule 3) or getting it right (rule 4). Keeping these rules will be a matter of established classroom culture – children will need to practise withholding judgement.

How can I use it?

Brainstorm when ideas are needed or problems have to be solved. A good place to brainstorm is in design and technology. PoS 1a asks children to *generate ideas for products after thinking about who will use them and what they will be used for . . .* A whole-class brainstorm will generate many viable products which individual children may not have found alone. When the ideas have been produced, another thinking tool can be used to evaluate them.

In the wider curriculum problems and issues arise – in the playground, lunch hall, between friends, in the classroom. Brainstorming can provide answers.

Show me, then!

Let's say that some children have been complaining about lunchtimes. After questioning them you discover that they have lost interest in the playtime games and have difficulty finding anything to do. You define the problem as 'How can we make lunchtimes more exciting?', establish the rules and begin a whole-class brainstorm. It could go like this:

> More games – Monopoly – animals – pets – friendship – mums and dads – food – crisps – books – football – toys – go home – shorter time – play with lunchtime supervisors – do jobs – help younger children – bouncy castle – go-karts – fairground rides – candy floss – toffee apples – apples – tuck shop – money – bank . . . and so on.

By allowing unworkable ideas and by not judging, a number of potential solutions appear.

Ask Tamara

Dear Tamara,

I want my pupils to learn effectively and make the best use of their brains. What advice would you give them?

Visionary, Portsmouth

Dear Visionary,

The main thing to understand about the brain is that it can only give out what gets put in. Therefore the best thing for any brain (adult and child alike) is stimulation. This can take many forms but the best idea is to vary the stimulation that the brain receives and to expose it to as many new or novel situations or ideas as possible. It may be something as simple as learning a new or unusual word every day or something more complex, such as learning about new cultures or religions through videos and films.

Exercising the brain can also help to improve functioning. Defining functioning is difficult, but quick and flexible thinking will be a bonus in any situation in adult life. Games can be used to help the child boost their memory and attention. An example is 'I went to grandma's house and I took with me . . . ' followed by a list of items – each suggested by a player; the children have to remember all the items in order.

Similarly, there are games that can be played in everyday life which might help children to be more attentive – for example asking the child to note which wrist the next five people they meet are wearing their watch on. These types of games can enhance attention – adults can try them too.

If these types of games are not suitable for a particular child, there is nothing to stop them from inventing their own games – even perhaps their own board game.

Whatever route you took to get to the end of this book, you will have discovered something to enhance the thinking and learning of your pupils. You have had the opportunity to think through your own teaching, then pick up a set of tools to enrich it. You have thought about where to think, what to think, who does the thinking and how they do it. And now it's time for action. By infusing any of the ideas in this book into what you already do, you will be helping to create a new way of teaching: a way that is preparing children for their futures as thinkers, problem solvers and creators.

As your teaching evolves, use some of the tools you have discovered to evaluate progress. Some ideas will work, others will need revision. You may begin to create new thinking tools of your own. Whatever the result, I should love to hear your thoughts. Tell me how you implement Thinking Classroom ideas and what your pupils' responses are. Please feel free to e-mail me at mike@aspiroweb.co.uk

How do you like to work and learn?

Imagine that you are learning something new.

Where

In the place where you learn,
do you like it to be:
Tick up to 4 boxes

Noisy (e.g. music/people talking)? . . . . . . ☐
Silent? . . . . ☐
Brightly lit? . . . . ☐
Dimly lit? . . . . ☐
Hot? . . . . ☐
Warm? . . . . ☐
Cool? . . . . ☐
Cold? . . . . ☐
Other? . . . . ☐

You

When you are learning, do you like to:
Tick up to 3 boxes

Sit at a desk? . . . . ☐
Sit in a comfy chair? . . . . ☐
Lie down on the floor/on a bean-bag? . . . ☐
Get up and walk about? . . . . ☐
Stay in one place? . . . . ☐
Other? . . . . ☐

Getting started, keeping going

Do you:
Tick up to 3 boxes

Find it is easy to start work? . . . . ☐
Need to think about it first? . . . . ☐
Need a teacher to get you to start? . . . . ☐
Always finish a job? . . . . ☐
Like to have short breaks? . . . . ☐

When

Do you like to learn:
Tick up to 3 boxes

Before school? . . . . ☐
Before morning playtime? . . . . ☐
After morning playtime? . . . . ☐
At lunchtime? . . . . ☐
After lunch? . . . . ☐
After school? . . . . ☐
In the evening? . . . . ☐
At bedtime? . . . . ☐
Other time? . . . . ☐

Your lessons

When you are learning, do you like:
Tick up to 6 boxes

To have time to think? . . . . ☐
To work alone? . . . . ☐
To work in pairs? . . . . ☐
To work in a team? . . . . ☐
To read? . . . . ☐
To listen? . . . . ☐
To see a picture or video? . . . . ☐
To talk to others? . . . . ☐
To write? . . . . ☐
To doodle? . . . . ☐
To fiddle? . . . . ☐
To move about? . . . . ☐
Other? . . . . ☐

Learning style assessment

Learning style profile for ....

Date ....

Work one to one, sitting face to face. As the learner imagines or says the answers to the questions below, observe how their eyes move. Concentrate on the eye movements, not the answers. Put a small cross on *one* of the eyes below to indicate where their eyes travel. If the eyes come to rest in more than one place for a question, make more than one cross. The distribution of crosses will indicate the spread of visual, auditory and kinaesthetic thinking. *This is only a starting point for right-handers and there will be exceptions.*

Spell 'hippopotamus'.	What's the first thing you said today?
Imagine the feel of rain.	What time did you go to bed last night?
Remember the sound of a motorbike.	Imagine your favourite pop song in your head.
Imagine the feel of clay on your hands.	Imagine the voice of a talking mouse.
Imagine the sound of a zip.	What was the weather like yesterday?
What is 123 X 4? (or another 'just too hard' calculation)	Imagine a blue dog with a green pig on its head.
What was the best part of your last holiday?	Imagine the sound of the school fire alarm.
Imagine the feel of a stomach ache.	How do you get to your house from here?
What's your favourite TV programme?	Remember the voice of a friend.
What do your favourite clothes look like?	How many classrooms are there in the school?

Thinking with Edward de Bono's Six Hats

Name . . . .

Date . . . .

I'm thinking about . . .

Boss

Facts

Feelings

Problems

Hopes

Ideas

Because of my thinking, I'm going to . . .

Bloomin' thinking

Find out — What? When? Where? Who? Which?

Understand — Can you explain? Can you describe? Can you tell me . . . ?

Make use of what you know — Can you use it in a different place?

Take it apart — What bits make the whole thing?

Put it together in another way — How could it be different/improved/developed?

Judge what happens — Is it as good as . . . ?

Thinking design

What are you going to design and make (your product)?

What do you already know?

How will you use what you know?

What are the different parts of your product?

What might be the problems in designing and making your product?

Are there any different ways to make your product?

How will you know if your design and product are successful?

Living graph

Traffic

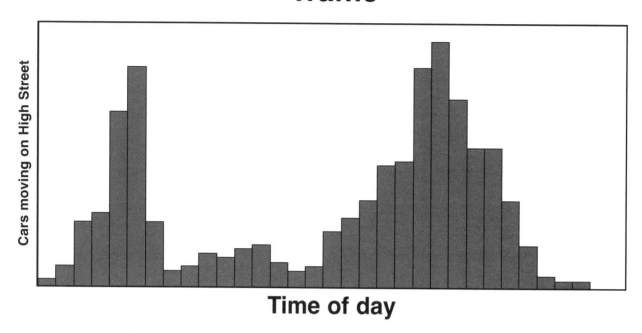

Time of day

The Woodhouse family lives in the High Street. Their son Tom goes to school in the same street. Here are ten facts about the Woodhouse family. Which bar on the graph above fits each fact the best? Write the fact number under the bar.

1. Sarah Woodhouse (age 3) and Mum go to meet Tom from school.
2. Mrs Woodhouse tells her son Tom to be careful crossing the road to school.
3. Tom's teacher closes the classroom window because the noise from the street is stopping the class thinking.
4. Mr Woodhouse feels angry because he is stuck in traffic on the way to work.
5. Sarah walks to playgroup with her mum.
6. Mr Woodhouse wakes up — it's quiet and dark.
7. Tom wakes up — it's noisy.
8. Mr and Mrs Woodhouse go to the cinema.
9. The babysitter arrives — she is late because of a traffic jam.
10. Tom and Sarah turn on the TV.

Memory team shapes

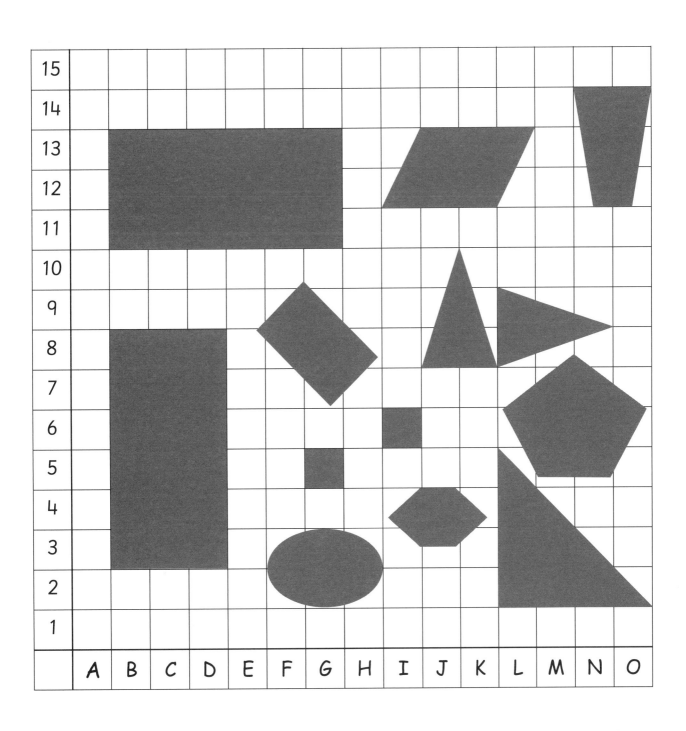

Thinking pictures

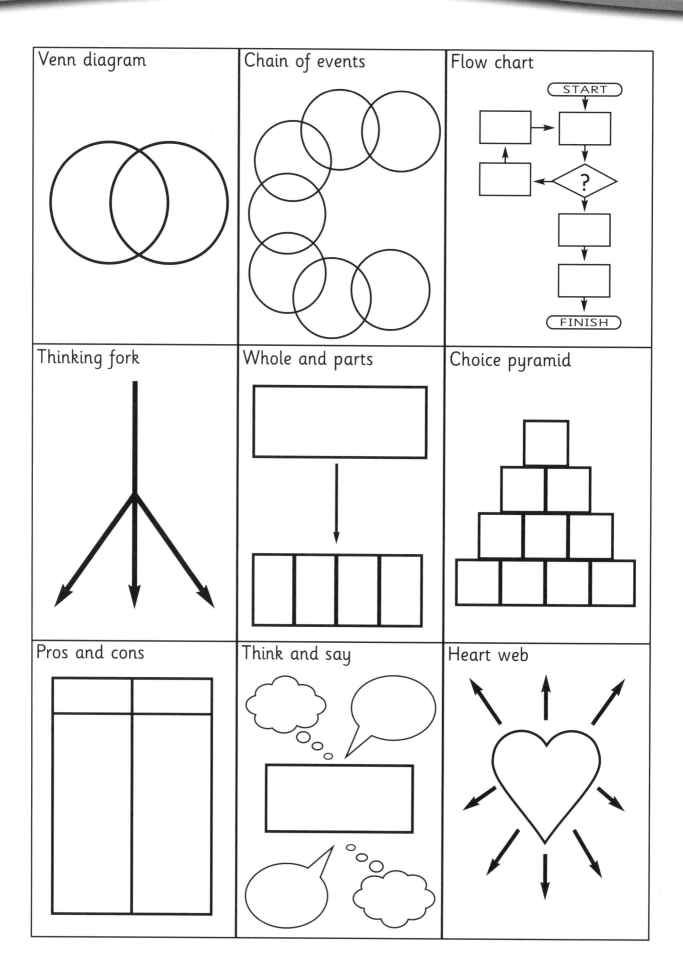

Venn diagram

Chain of events

Flow chart

START

?

FINISH

Thinking fork

Whole and parts

Choice pyramid

Pros and cons

Think and say

Heart web

Suggestions for using thinking pictures

Venn diagram
Use it for: Classifying
For example: English

Exploring story characters:
- Put attributes which only character A has in one circle.
- Put attributes which only character B has in the other.
- Put shared attributes in the intersection.
- Put attributes which neither A nor B has outside both circles.

Chain of events
Use it for: Sequencing
For example: Science

Feeding relationships:
- Chain links represent the connection of ideas.
- Write or draw prey in first link.
- Write or draw its predator in adjoining link.
- Write or draw the next predator in the following link and so on.

Flow chart
Use it for: Planning and evaluating
For example: Design and technology

Testing a product:
- Put processes in rectangles; e.g. 1st rectangle: test product.
- Put questions in diamond shapes; does it meet requirement?
- Follow different paths depending on the answer; if yes, finish write up; if no, make adjustments/retest.

Thinking fork
Use it for: Predicting
For example: History

Enquiry:
- Put a question on the handle: 'Why did the Romans invade Britain?'
- Put possible answers on tines:
  – 'Because they wanted a colder climate.'
  – 'To expand their empire.'
  – 'To steal land, animals and money.'
  – Seek evidence.

Whole and parts
Use it for: Planning
For example: Music

Composing and performing:
- Put the task in the top box: 'Compose and perform a short animal piece.'
- Put four sub-tasks in the boxes at the bottom:
  – 'Choose animal/instruments.'
  – 'Create piece.'
  – 'Rehearse and adapt.'
  – 'Perform and evaluate.'

Choice pyramid
Use it for: Making decisions
For example: Geography

Enquiry and skills:
- From four possibilities, eliminate three until the best option remains.
  'With limited resources, what action would you take to reduce river pollution?'
- Four ideas on bottom row.
- Remove one to give next row.
- Remove another for next row.
- Remove third to give best idea, which sits at the top.

Pros and cons
Use it for: Comparing
For example: Mathematics

Calculation methods:
- Consider mental vs paper and pencil methods.
- List the pros of mental: quick, no materials needed, can do it anywhere.
- List cons of mental: limited size of numbers, no record.
- Repeat for paper and pencil methods.

Think and say
Use it for: Reflecting
For example: Art

Evaluating/developing work:
- View either a range of stimulus material or a range of completed work.
- Choose one piece.
- Write its title in the rectangle.
- Write comments about piece in speech bubbles.
- Write thoughts about piece in thought bubbles.
- Consider differences between thoughts/speech.

Heart web
Use it for: Finding solutions
For example: PE

Dance activity:
- Write dance theme in the heart, e.g. war.
- Become aware of feelings about the dance theme – scared, confident, excited, worried.
- Develop movements for each feeling.
- Join movements to create dance.

Which one is the odd one out?

English

Adjectives

| lucky | interesting | lottery | fortunate |

Characters

| giant | Dumbledore | witch | princess |

Authors

| Roald Dahl | Jacqueline Wilson | Alan Ahlberg | Michael Rosen |

Punctuation marks

| . | , | ! | ? |

Mathematics

Shape

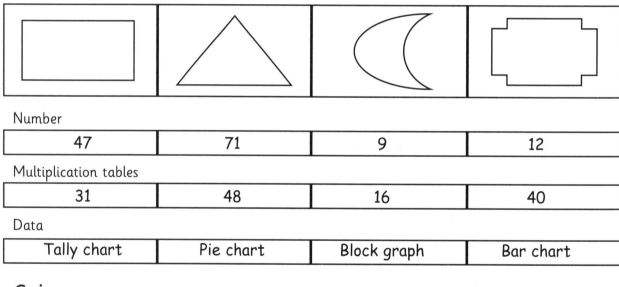

Number

| 47 | 71 | 9 | 12 |

Multiplication tables

| 31 | 48 | 16 | 40 |

Data

| Tally chart | Pie chart | Block graph | Bar chart |

Science

Nutrition

| cake | bread | carrot | sausage |

Light

| wood | metal | glass | torch |

PE

Games

| football | tennis | ice-hockey | swimming |

Geography

Locational knowledge

| London | Birmingham | Edinburgh | Dublin |